# THE SMALL HANDS OF SLAVERY

## Bonded Child Labor In India

### Human Rights Watch Children's Rights Project

### Human Rights Watch/Asia

**Human Rights Watch**
New York • Washington • London • Brussels

ISBN 1-56432-172-X
Library of Congress Catalog Card Number 96-77536

Cover photograph © December 1995 by Arvind Ganesan. A young girl working as a bonded laborer in the silk reeling process in Karnataka. All photographs in this report by Arvind Ganesan.

*Human Rights Watch Children's Rights Project*
The Human Rights Watch Children's Rights Project was established in 1994 to monitor and promote the human rights of children around the world. Lois Whitman is the director, Yodon Thonden is counsel, Lee Tucker, Rosa Ehrenreich, and Arvind Ganesan are consultants. Jane Green Schaller is chair of the Advisory Committee.

*Human Rights Watch/Asia*
Human Rights Watch/Asia was established in 1985 to monitor and promote the observance of internationally recognized human rights in Asia. Sidney Jones is the executive director; Mike Jendrzejczyk is the Washington director; Robin Munro is the Hong Kong director; Patricia Gossman is senior researcher; Jeannine Guthrie is NGO Liaison; Dinah PoKempner is counsel; Zunetta Liddell is research associate; Joyce Wan is Henry R. Luce Fellow; Paul Lall and Olga Nousias are associates; Mickey Spiegel is research consultant. Andrew J. Nathan is chair of the advisory committee and Orville Schell is vice chair.

Addresses for Human Rights Watch
485 Fifth Avenue, New York, NY 10017-6104
Tel: (212) 972-8400, Fax: (212) 972-0905, E-mail: hrwnyc@hrw.org

1522 K Street, N.W., #910, Washington, DC 20005-1202
Tel: (202) 371-6592, Fax: (202) 371-0124, E-mail: hrwdc@hrw.org

33 Islington High Street, N1 9LH London, UK
Tel: (171) 713-1995, Fax: (171) 713-1800, E-mail: hrwatchuk@gn.apc.org

15 Rue Van Campenhout, 1000 Brussels, Belgium
Tel: (2) 732-2009, Fax: (2) 732-0471, E-mail: hrwatcheu@gn.apc.org

Website Address: http://www.hrw.org
Gopher Address://gopher.humanrights.org:5000
Listserv address: To subscribe to the list, send an e-mail message to majordomo@igc.apc.org with "subscribe hrw-news" in the body of the message (leave the subject line blank).

# HUMAN RIGHTS WATCH

Human Rights Watch conducts regular, systematic investigations of human rights abuses in some seventy countries around the world. Our reputation for timely, reliable disclosures has made us an essential source of information for those concerned with human rights. We address the human rights practices of governments of all political stripes, of all geopolitical alignments, and of all ethnic and religious persuasions. Human Rights Watch defends freedom of thought and expression, due process and equal protection of the law, and a vigorous civil society; we document and denounce murders, disappearances, torture, arbitrary imprisonment, discrimination, and other abuses of internationally recognized human rights. Our goal is to hold governments accountable if they transgress the rights of their people.

Human Rights Watch began in 1978 with the founding of its Helsinki division. Today, it includes five divisions covering Africa, the Americas, Asia, the Middle East, as well as the signatories of the Helsinki accords. It also includes three collaborative projects on arms transfers, children's rights, and women's rights. It maintains offices in New York, Washington, Los Angeles, London, Brussels, Moscow, Dushanbe, Rio de Janeiro, and Hong Kong. Human Rights Watch is an independent, nongovernmental organization, supported by contributions from private individuals and foundations worldwide. It accepts no government funds, directly or indirectly.

The staff includes Kenneth Roth, executive director; Cynthia Brown, program director; Holly J. Burkhalter, advocacy director; Barbara Guglielmo, finance and administration director; Robert Kimzey, publications director; Jeri Laber, special advisor; Lotte Leicht, Brussels office director; Juan Méndez, general counsel; Susan Osnos, communications director; Jemera Rone, counsel; and Joanna Weschler, United Nations representative.

The regional directors of Human Rights Watch are Peter Takirambudde, Africa; José Miguel Vivanco, Americas; Sidney Jones, Asia; Holly Cartner, Helsinki; and Eric Goldstein (acting), Middle East. The project directors are Joost R. Hiltermann, Arms Project; Lois Whitman, Children's Rights Project; and Dorothy Q. Thomas, Women's Rights Project.

The members of the board of directors are Robert L. Bernstein, chair; Adrian W. DeWind, vice chair; Roland Algrant, Lisa Anderson, William Carmichael, Dorothy Cullman, Gina Despres, Irene Diamond, Edith Everett, Jonathan Fanton, James C. Goodale, Jack Greenberg, Vartan Gregorian, Alice H. Henkin, Stephen L. Kass, Marina Pinto Kaufman, Bruce Klatsky, Harold Hongju Koh, Alexander MacGregor, Josh Mailman, Samuel K. Murumba, Andrew Nathan, Jane Olson, Peter Osnos, Kathleen Peratis, Bruce Rabb, Sigrid Rausing, Orville Schell, Sid Sheinberg, Gary G. Sick, Malcolm Smith, Domna Stanton, Nahid Toubia, Maureen White, and Rosalind C. Whitehead.

## ACKNOWLEDGMENTS

The Human Rights Watch Children's Rights Project and Human Rights Watch/Asia are indebted to numerous individuals and organizations for their valuable and generous assistance in the course of researching this report. We thank the following: Belgian journalists Rudi Rotthier and Marleen Daniels; Mike Dottridge of Anti-Slavery International; author and researcher Neera Burra; Joseph Gathia of the Centre of Concern for Child Labour; Hamida Habibullah of the Indian Council on Child Welfare; Shamshad Khan of the Centre for Rural Education and Development Action; J.P. Solomon of the Campaign Against Child Labour, Bangalore; Ratan Katyayni of Mukti Dhara Sansthan; U.R. Mohnot of Centre for Concern for Child Labour; Ossie Fernandes of the Human Rights Advocacy and Research Foundation; Felix Sugirtharaj of the Association for the Rural Poor; M. Siraj Sait, Advocate; Swami Agnivesh of the Bonded Labour Liberation Front; Colin Gonzalves, Advocate; Kiran Kamal Prasad of JEEVIKA; and Kailash Satyarthi of the South Asian Coalition Against Child Servitude.

We also thank the many people who prefer, for reasons of their own well-being and that of their organizations, that their names not be mentioned. This list would be significantly longer than the list above—an unfortunate indicator of the volatility surrounding the issue of child labor in India. Finally, we thank and honor the many brave children who spoke with us, recounting their personal experiences of hardship and bondage. They made this report possible.

This report was written by Lee Tucker, a consultant to Human Rights Watch, and is based on research conducted by Ms. Tucker and Arvind Ganesan, also a consultant to Human Rights Watch, from November 1995 through January 1996. Mr. Ganesan also provided additional research and contributed to the writing of Chapter V. Jeannine Guthrie, NGO Liaison for Human Rights Watch/Asia provided additional research assistance. The report was edited by Lois Whitman, director of the Human Rights Watch Children's Rights Project, Patricia Gossman, senior researcher for Human Rights Watch/Asia, Sidney Jones, executive director of Human Rights Watch/Asia, and Michael McClintock, deputy program director of Human Rights Watch. Production assistance was provided by Paul Lall and Olga Nousias, Human Rights Watch/Asia associates.

Shame upon such crimes!
Shame upon us if we do not raise our voices against them!

Samuel Gompers, U.S. labor activist, 1881

# CONTENTS

# I. SUMMARY

*My sister is ten years old. Every morning at seven she goes to the bonded labor man, and every night at nine she comes home. He treats her badly; he hits her if he thinks she is working slowly or if she talks to the other children, he yells at her, he comes looking for her if she is sick and cannot go to work. I feel this is very difficult for her.*

*I don't care about school or playing. I don't care about any of that. All I want is to bring my sister home from the bonded labor man. For 600 rupees I can bring her home—that is our only chance to get her back.*

*We don't have 600 rupees . . . we will never have 600 rupees.*

—Lakshmi,[1] nine year-old beedi (cigarette) roller, Tamil Nadu. Six hundred rupees is the equivalent of approximately $17.[2]

*******

With credible estimates ranging from 60 to 115 million, India has the largest number of working children in the world. Whether they are sweating in the heat of stone quarries, working in the fields sixteen hours a day, picking rags in city streets, or hidden away as domestic servants, these children endure miserable and difficult lives. They earn little and are abused much. They struggle to make enough to eat and perhaps to help feed their families as well. They do not go to school; more than half of them will never learn the barest skills of literacy. Many of them have been working since the age of four or five, and by the time they reach adulthood they may be irrevocably sick or deformed—they will certainly be exhausted, old men and women by the age of forty, likely to be dead by fifty.

Most or all of these children are working under some form of compulsion, whether from their parents, from the expectations attached to their caste, or from simple economic necessity. At least fifteen million of them, however, are working

---

[1] All names have been changed.

[2] All dollar amounts refer to U.S. dollars.

1

as virtual slaves.[3] These are the bonded child laborers of India. This report is about them.

"Bonded child labor" refers to the phenomenon of children working in conditions of servitude in order to pay off a debt.[4] The debt that binds them to their employer is incurred not by the children themselves, but by their relatives or guardians—usually by a parent. In India, these debts tend to be relatively modest, ranging on average from 500 rupees to 7,500 rupees,[5] depending on the industry and the age and skill of the child. The creditors-cum-employers offer these "loans" to destitute parents in an effort to secure the labor of a child, which is always cheap, but even cheaper under a situation of bondage. The parents, for their part, accept the loans. Bondage is a traditional worker-employer relationship in India, and the parents need the money—perhaps to pay for the costs of an illness, perhaps to provide a dowry to a marrying child, or perhaps—as is often the case—to help put food on the table.

---

[3] The estimate of fifteen million bonded child laborers is conservative. Anti-Slavery International reported in 1991 that India had fifteen million bonded child laborers working in agriculture alone. Anti-Slavery International, *Children in Bondage: Slaves of the Subcontinent* (London: 1991), p. 30. Given that agriculture accounts for approximately 52 to 87 percent of all bonded child laborers (see chapter on agriculture), there could be millions more working in non-agricultural occupations. "Indians form panel to stop child labor," United Press International, November 18, 1994. Other activists and academics estimate that one quarter of all working children, that is, between fifteen and twenty-nine million, are bonded laborers. Based on these and other coinciding estimates, Human Rights Watch considers fifteen million to be a reliable minimum indicator of the prevalence of bonded child labor in India.

[4] The United Nations Supplementary Convention on the Abolition of Slavery, the Slave Trade, and Institutions and Practices Similar to Slavery, 1956, defines debt bondage as "the status or condition arising from a pledge by a debtor of his personal services or those of a person under his control as security for a debt, if the value of those services as reasonably assessed is not applied towards the liquidation of the debt or the length and nature of those services are not respectively limited and defined." It should be noted that many Indian activists consider all child labor to be a form of bondage, given the child's powerlessness and inability to *freely* choose to work. This report, however, considers bonded child labor to be that which conforms to the definition of the U.N. Supplementary Convention.

[5] Between $15 and $220, at the late 1995 exchange rate of thirty-four rupees to the U.S. dollar.

The children who are sold to these bond masters work long hours over many years in an attempt to pay off these debts. Due to the astronomically high rates of interest charged and the abysmally low wages paid, they are usually unsuccessful. As they reach maturity, some of them may be released by the employer in favor of a newly-indebted and younger child. Many others will pass the debt on, intact or even higher, to a younger sibling, back to a parent, or on to their own children.

The past few years have seen increasing public awareness—in India itself, but particularly in the international arena—of the high incidence of child servitude in the carpet industry of South Asia. As a consequence, the international public has come to associate "child servitude" with the image of small children chained to carpet looms, slaving away over the thousands of tiny wool knots that will eventually become expensive carpets in the homes of the wealthy. International concern for the carpet weavers reached a peak in April 1995, when children's rights activist Iqbal Masih, a twelve-year-old ex-carpet weaver in Pakistan, was murdered.[6]

This attention and the outrage it has provoked are entirely warranted—the use of bonded child labor in the production of carpets for export is extensive, and conditions in that industry are horrendous.[7] But it is vital that the public's concern for children in servitude not begin and end with carpets. More than 300,000 children are estimated to be working in the carpet industry,[8] the majority of them in bondage. This is a large number, but it represents only about 2 percent of the bonded child laborers of India.

The great majority of the carpet weavers' bonded brothers and sisters are working in the agricultural sector, tending cattle and goats, picking tea leaves on vast plantations, and working fields of sugar cane and basic crops all across the

---

[6] Iqbal Masih was shot and killed on April 16, 1995. Initially blamed on the carpet industrialists of Pakistan, the murder was later attributed to a villager whom Masih reportedly discovered involved in an illicit act.

[7] See chapter on handwoven carpets.

[8] Neera Burra, *Born to Work: Child Labour in India* (New Delhi: Oxford University Press, 1995), p. xxii.

country. Apart from agriculture, which accounts for 64 percent[9] of all labor in India, bonded child laborers form a significant part of the work force in a multitude of domestic and export industries. These include, but are not limited to, the production of silk and silk saris, beedi (hand-rolled cigarettes), silver jewelry, synthetic gemstones, leather products (including footwear and sporting goods), handwoven wool carpets, and precious gemstones and diamonds. Services where bonded child labor is prevalent include prostitution, small restaurants, truck stops and tea shop services, and domestic servitude.

The practice of child debt servitude has been illegal in India since 1933, when the Children (Pledging of Labour) Act was enacted under British rule. Since independence, a plethora of additional protective legislation has been put in place. There are distinct laws governing child labor in factories, in commercial establishments, on plantations, and in apprenticeships. There are laws governing the use of migrant labor and contract labor. A relatively recent law—the Child Labour (Prohibition and Regulation) Act of 1986—designates a child as "a person who has not completed their fourteenth year of age."[10] It purports to regulate the hours and conditions of some child workers and to prohibit the use of child labor in certain enumerated hazardous industries. (There is no blanket prohibition on the use of child labor, nor any universal minimum age set for child workers.)[11] Most important of all, for children in servitude, is the Bonded Labour System (Abolition) Act, 1976 which strictly outlaws all forms of debt bondage and forced labor. These extensive legal safeguards mean little, however, without the political will to implement them. In India, this will is sorely lacking. All of the labor laws are

---

[9] Ministry of Labour, *Annual Report 1994-95* (New Delhi: Government of India, 1995), p. 95. The actual quote is: "Out of India's total workforce of 314 million, about 80% (249 million) are in rural areas. About 64% of the workers (200 million) are engaged in agriculture. About 85% of the workers (267 million) are self-employed or on casual wages. Only about 15% (47 million) have regular salaried employment."

[10] Child Labour (Prohibition and Regulation) Act, 1986, Part I, Section 2(ii).

[11] There is no universal definition of a child under Indian law. The Child Labour (Prohibition and Regulation) Act, 1986, the Minimum Wages Act, 1948, the Plantation Labour Act, 1951, the Apprentices Act, 1961, and Article 24 of the Indian Constitution define "child" as any person under the age of fourteen. The Shops and Establishments Act, 1961 allows the definition to be set by the states and in thirteen states, the minimum age is twelve, and in eleven states, the minimum age is fourteen. The Children (Pledging of Labour) Act, 1993 defines a child as anyone below the age of fifteen. The Juvenile Justice Act, 1986 defines "juveniles" as any male under sixteen or any female under eighteen.

routinely flouted, and with virtually no risk of punishment to the offender. Whether due to corruption or indifference—and both are much in evidence—these laws are simply not enforced. In those rare cases where offenders are prosecuted, sentences are limited to negligible fines.

Why does India—the Indian government, the ruling elite, the business interests, the populace as a whole—tolerate this slavery in its midst? According to a vast and deeply entrenched set of myths, bonded labor and child labor in India are inevitable. They are caused by poverty. They represent the natural order of things, and it is not possible to change them by force; they must evolve slowly toward eradication.[12]

In truth, the Indian government has failed to protect its most vulnerable children. When others have stepped in to try to fill the vacuum and advocate on behalf of those children, India's leaders and much of its media have attributed nearly all "outside" attempts at action to an ulterior commercial motive. The developed world is not concerned with Indian children, this view holds, but rather with maintaining a competitive lead in the global marketplace. Holding to this defensive stance, some officials have threatened to end all foreign funding of child labor-related projects.

This nationalist rhetoric has been largely a diversionary tactic. What the government has hoped to hide is the news that, no matter how the data are analyzed, official efforts to end the exploitation of child laborers are woefully deficient. Former Prime Minister P. V. Narasimha Rao, for example, made much of his initiative, announced in 1994, to bring two million children out of hazardous employment by the year 2000. Two million represents only 1.7 to 3.3 percent of the nation's child laborers; the fate of the other 58 to 113 million children was not addressed. In a welcome move, the United Front government, elected in May 1996, has promised to eradicate child labor in all occupations and industries, and has stated that the right to free compulsory elementary education should be made a

---

[12] Bonded child labor is convenient, cheap, compliant, and dependable. It depresses wages. It is easily replenishable. Bonded labor among both adults and children is not a new phenomenon in India. It is an old arrangement, and a convenient one for the lucky top layers of privilege. Those who have the power to change this arrangement are, by all measures, uninterested in doing so.

fundamental right and enforced through suitable statutory measures.[13] It remains to be seen what measures the government will take to fulfill these promises.

By focusing primarily on child labor in export industries and the threat of sanctions on exports, the international community has sent the unfortunate message that only child labor in export industries must be addressed. In response, the Indian government has accused its international critics of protectionism and has adopted superficial remedies designed to assuage their concerns while continuing to ignore its legal obligation to identify, release and rehabilitate bonded laborers.

Multilateral lending institutions have failed in their obligations as well. By neglecting to ensure that the projects they fund do not involve the use of bonded child labor, they have exacerbated the problem of bonded child labor. These institutions, and their funders should take every measure to ensure that aid does not result in child slavery.

This report, based on two months of field investigations, reveals only a glimpse of the vast suffering caused by the bonded labor system. This glimpse alone, however, is proof enough that it is time for India's new government to accept responsibility for the slavery in its midst, to admit that it is not inevitable, and to end it. India is the world's largest democracy, a nuclear power, the world's second most populous country, and, although a poor nation, one of the six largest economies of the world. It is possible to end child servitude. The only thing lacking is will.

*******

This report is the result of an investigation conducted by two Human Rights Watch researchers from November 1995 to January 1996. More than one hundred bonded child laborers were interviewed. Children were chosen for interviews on the basis of their willingness and ability to speak freely with researchers; no interviews were conducted in the presence of employers or in circumstances that presented the risk of retaliation. In addition to the children, Human Rights Watch spoke with more than fifty government officials, employers, social workers, community activists, attorneys, and religious leaders. Some of the government officials interviewed requested that their comments be kept off the record and many human rights activists requested anonymity. These requests, which highlight the sensitive nature of the issue of child bondage, have been

---

[13] United Front Coalition's Economic Program, presented June 6, 1996, pp. 3-4. From *MakroIndia Business Page* sponsored by Amrok Securities Private Limited at *www.macroindia.com/hlight1.htm.*

honored.   The investigation took place in the states of Tamil Nadu, Karnataka, Rajasthan, Maharashtra, and Uttar Pradesh.

While India leads the world in the number of bonded child laborers, debt servitude is a significant problem in Pakistan and Nepal as well.[14]   Nor are contemporary forms of slavery confined to South Asia; previous Human Rights Watch reports have documented forced labor in Kuwait, Brazil, Thailand, and the Dominican Republic.[15]   Regarding India, a prior Human Rights Watch report documented slavery-like conditions in Bombay brothels.[16]

---

[14]   See Human Rights Watch/Asia, *Contemporary Forms of Slavery in Pakistan* (New York: Human Rights Watch, July 1995); Anti-Slavery International, *Children in Bondage: Slaves of the Subcontinent* (London: Anti-Slavery International, 1991); INSEC, *Bonded Labour in Nepal under Kamaiya System* (Kathmandu: INSEC, 1992); and *Report of the Working Group on Contemporary Forms of Slavery* (18th Session, June 1993), UN DOC E/CN.4/1993/67.

[15]   Asia Watch and Human Rights Watch Women's Rights Project, *A Modern Form of Slavery: Trafficking of Women and Girls into Brothels in Thailand* (New York: Human Rights Watch, 1993); Americas Watch, "Forced Labor in Brazil Revisited," vol. 5, no. 12, November, 1993; Middle East Watch and Human Rights Watch Women's Rights Project, "Rape and Mistreatment of Asian Maids in Kuwait," vol. 4, no. 8, July 1992; Americas Watch, *The Struggle for Land in Brazil: Rural Violence Continues* (New York: Human Rights Watch, 1992); Americas Watch, "Forced Labor in Brazil," vol. 2, no. 8, December 1990; and National Coalition for Haitian Refugees, Americas Watch, and Caribbean Rights, *Harvesting Oppression: Forced Haitian Labor in the Dominican Sugar Industry* (New York: Human Rights Watch, 1990).

[16]   Human Rights Watch/Asia, *Rape for Profit: Trafficking of Nepali Girls and Women to India's Brothels* (New York: Human Rights Watch, June 1995).

## II. RECOMMENDATIONS

**Recommendations to the Government of India**

The government of India should demonstrate its commitment to the eradication of bonded child labor by implementing the following recommendations at the earliest possible date:

**General Recommendations**

- Design and implement a multi-pronged effort to end bonded child labor, composed of both persuasive and mandatory means. At a minimum, this effort should include stepped-up enforcement efforts, free, compulsory, and quality public education, and financial support for children to go to school.

- Implement measures designed to bring current practice into compliance with Article 45 of the constitution which mandates free and compulsory education for all children up to fourteen years of age.

- Pressure states and districts to constitute and oversee bonded labor vigilance committees, as required by the Bonded Labour (System) Abolition Act, 1976. Ensure that a sufficient number of investigators can be included in the committee to guarantee implementation of the act. Given the massive numbers of children involved, nongovernmental organization (NGO) representatives, lawyers, social workers, teachers, civil servants, and others with ties to bonded laborers and their families should be enlisted as investigators. Provide in-depth training to district officials charged with enforcing the act, as directed by the Supreme Court in *Neeraja Chaudhary v. State of Madhya Pradesh*, 1984.

- Establish an independent monitoring agency at the state and national level to oversee the enforcement of the Bonded Labour (System Abolition) Act, 1976. For full implementation of the Act, this body should be statutorily empowered to receive and address complaints of Act violations and complaints of official misconduct. It should also be able to file First Information Reports (FIRs), the first step in prosecution of a criminal charge, when bonded child laborers are identified.

- Establish a similar independent monitoring agency to oversee the enforcement of the Child Labour (Prohibition and Regulation) Act, 1986.

- Ensure the active involvement of the Scheduled Castes and Scheduled Tribes Commission in the process of identifying, releasing, and rehabilitating bonded child laborers.

- Establish and make public a master list or national register of children released from bondage, including how they were rehabilitated (provided with schooling, vocational training, or other alternative measures).

- Establish and make public a master list or national register of people prosecuted under the Bonded Labour (System Abolition) Act, 1976 and the Child Labour (Prohibition and Regulation) Act, 1986 and include information on the nature of sentences given to guilty parties.

- Establish and make public up-to-date and accurate information regarding the incidence and distribution of bonded child laborers, and the industries in which such children work.

- Investigate the abuse and exploitation of children by agents and employers, and prosecute such agents and employers under the relevant domestic law such as Chapter VI of the Juvenile Justice Act, or Chapter XVI of the Indian Penal Code.

- Condition all entitlements, subsidies, special tax allowances, and other concessions currently extended to industries that employ bonded child labor on compliance with the Bonded Labour System (Abolition) Act, 1976 and other relevant laws.

- Condition all new subsidies and incentives on industry compliance with applicable domestic laws banning bonded labor.

- Launch a nationwide public awareness campaign regarding the legal prohibition of bonded child labor. This campaign should explain in simple terms what actions are legally prohibited and what recourses and resources are available to bonded child laborers and their families.

- Amend relevant legislation, including the Child Labour (Prohibition and Regulation) Act, to bring it into compliance with the requirements of the Indian Constitution.

- Add to the Bonded Labour System (Abolition) Act and the Child Labour (Prohibition and Regulation) Act additional punishments for violators, including forfeiture of operating licenses, seizure of manufacturing equipment, and short and long-term closure of plants. Amend the Bonded Labour System (Abolition) Act, 1976 to significantly increase fines and allow the fines to be paid as compensation to the freed bonded laborers. Amend Section 10 to require all employers to have and show on demand proof of age of all children working on their premises. Failure to have adequate proof should constitute a separate violation of the act. In the event of a dispute regarding a child's age, the burden of proof should be on the employer to prove that the child is above the age of fourteen years.

- Amend the Child Labour (Prohibition and Regulation) Act, 1986 so that household enterprises and government schools and training centers are no longer exempted for prohibitions on employing children; rules formulated by the central government will apply until replaced by rules formulated by the states themselves; and coverage under the act should be expanded to include agriculture and informal sectors.

- Amend the Beedi and Cigar Workers Act so that exemptions for household-based production are eliminated.

- Amend the Children (Pledging of Labour) Act so that fines to employers, agents, and creditors are increased, the funds collected are contributed to the compensation and rehabilitation of the children exploited; imprisonment as a sentencing alternative is added; and specify which governmental department is responsible for enforcement of this act.

- Amend the Factories Act to cover all factories or workshops employing child labor, not just those with twenty or more workers, or ten or more workers where power is used.

- Meet International Labour Organisation norms of one Ministry of Labour inspector for every 150 factories and establishments.

- Amend the Trade Union Act to allow children to form and participate in trade unions as an interim measure pending the elimination of bonded child labor. The Convention on the Rights of the Child, which India has ratified guarantees the children the right of freedom of association.

- Promptly submit the Indian government's report on compliance with the Convention on the Rights of the Child to the United Nations Committee on the Rights of the Child, as this has been overdue for more than one year.

- Continue cooperation with international organizations working to abolish bonded child labor, in particular the International Labour Organisation's International Programme to Eliminate Child Labour

**Recommendations to United Nations Agencies**

- The United Nations Working Group on Contemporary Forms of Slavery should press the United Nations Human Rights Commission to examine the government of India's compliance with international laws and standards outlawing bonded labor, and to censure non-compliance. As a step toward ending bonded labor in India, Human Rights Watch recommends that the working group undertake a fact-finding mission to India and make recommendations designed to eliminate bonded labor.

- The ILO should send a technical mission to India to make recommendations with the understanding that India would develop an action plan for abolishing bonded child labor over a specific time period, either through the International Program to Eliminate Child Labor (IPEC) or other ILO programs.

- UNICEF should make the elimination of bonded child labor a stated priority of its efforts in India and elsewhere. It should formulate a consistent institutional policy regarding bonded child labor, and work with local, state, and national government officials toward the achievement of the stated goals.

- WHO should investigate and publicize the adverse health consequences for children of bonded child labor, and promote measures to eliminate the exposure of children to hazardous conditions and labor practices.

- WHO should formulate a policy on the elimination of bonded child labor, and collaborate with other UN agencies toward this end.

**Recommendations to the World Bank and Other International Lending Institutions**

- Condition receipt of loans and other subsidies on verified compliance with all domestic legal prohibitions on the use of bonded and child labor.

- Suspend the flow of aid to the sericulture (silk) industry until the government of India has taken concrete steps to identify, eradicate, and rehabilitate children in bondage.

- Prior to approval of projects, investigate the effect of proposed policies and programs on the incidence of child servitude.

- Provide funding for a program with NGOs and the Indian government to effectively implement India's Bonded Labour System (Abolition) Act, and to assist in identifying, releasing, and rehabilitating bonded child laborers, with a priority on industries which have previously received aid. Establish an institutionalized mechanism for incorporating local NGO ideas and opinions into projects at all stages of the decision making process—before a loan is released, while the project is being implemented, and in the course of any post-project evaluation.

**Recommendations to the International Community**

- India's international donors should suspend funding for any projects, such as sericulture, that are known to employ bonded child labor unless the project includes specific programs for the elimination of bonded child labor, education and rehabilitation of the affected children, and for improving the social welfare of the children and their families.

- Donors should explore the possibility of funding a program with NGOs and the Indian government to effectively implement India's Bonded Labor (Abolition) Act and accompanying rehabilitation scheme.

- Trade benefits provided under the Generalized System of Preferences in both the United States and in Europe are prohibited to countries where forced labor is tolerated. Accordingly, Human Rights Watch/Asia calls upon the United States Trade Representative and the European Union to initiate an investigation into the use of bonded child labor in India and into the Indian Government's enforcement of the Bonded Labour System (Abolition) Act, 1976. India's trading partners should use the leverage of

GSP trade benefits to encourage the government to eradicate bonded child labor and to provide rehabilitation and education to the children involved.

## Recommendations to Retailers, Suppliers, and Indian and International Consumers

- When making purchases from industries known to employ large numbers of children in bonded labor, such as the silk, carpet, beedi, silver, leather and agricultural sectors, consumers in India and abroad should require their retailers to pledge to reject goods from suppliers which employ bonded child labor in the manufacture of these goods and to support a good faith program to phase children out of bondage, offering them financial assistance and access to formal education. Consumers should also require retailers to guarantee that they and their suppliers offer full access to independent monitors to all facilities and supplier facilities to check on the incidence of bonded child labor.

- Corporations should incorporate a monitoring process for bonded child labor into their quality control procedures and in setting standards for selecting suppliers and products.

- Indian consumers should appeal to their members of the legislative assembly (MLA), district magistrates, and district collectors to demand that vigilance committees be established and strengthened, and demand that the government of India identify, release, and rehabilitate all bonded laborers (including children) as required under the Bonded Labour (Abolition) Act, 1976, and accompanying rehabilitation scheme.

- International consumers should appeal to their own governments to press the Government of India to abide by its own law by administering in good faith the Bonded Labour (Abolition) Act, 1976, and accompanying procedures for the identification, release, and rehabilitation of bonded laborers.

## III. THE CONTEXT OF BONDED CHILD LABOR

It is commonly asserted that poverty is the cause of bonded and other forms of child labor. In fact, poverty is only one of many factors at play in creating and sustaining the conditions that facilitate endemic bondage.

In India, other key elements behind bonded child labor include: an ancient tradition of slavery and debt bondage; the lack of alternative small-scale loans for the rural and urban poor and the lack of a concerted social welfare scheme to safeguard against hunger and illness; a noncompulsory and unequal educational system; the lack of employment opportunities and living wages for adults; corruption and indifference among government officials; and societal apathy. A final element is caste-based discrimination, which is closely intertwined particularly with agricultural debt bondage.

*******

A new economic policy introduced in 1991 is transforming the Indian economy, supporting a burgeoning middle class and a thin layer of the ultra rich. The liberalization package includes lower import duties, access for foreign investors to India's growing industrial sector, privatization of previously state-run industries and services, and increased competition. India's total exports, valued at twenty-six billion U.S. dollars in 1994[17] (most of this in consumer goods), are expected to triple by the year 2000, pushing India into fourth place among the world's largest economies. (With over 900 million inhabitants, in 1996 India was the second largest country in terms of population.)

The benefit to the poor and working classes—who comprise a large majority of India's population—is less clear. Along with economic liberalization has come a structural adjustment program, and, according to many Indians, the repercussions of structural adjustment are battering the poor. The cost of living is rising in both urban and rural areas. Unemployment among adults remains high, with more than fifty-five million estimated to be jobless.[18] In the informal sector, which employs 85 percent of Indian workers,[19] including children, work conditions

---

[17] All dollar amounts in this report are in U.S. dollars.

[18] Pradeep Mehta, "Cashing in on Child Labor," *Multinational Monitor*, April 1994.

[19] Ministry of Labour, *Annual Report 1994-95*, p. 95.

are widely considered to be worsening, and the rate of bonded child labor is actually rising.[20]

This trend was noted in a 1995 report by the government-appointed Commission on Labour Standards and International Trade. According to the commission, child labor has been increasing in India at the rate of 4 percent a year, "while the working conditions of the children have remained unchanged, if not deteriorated."[21] Workers and social activists interviewed by Human Rights Watch across India confirmed this trend.

Social scientists estimate the number of India's working children to be between sixty and 115 million.[22] About 85 percent of these children work in the agricultural sector; the rest work in small-scale industries and the service sector,

---

[20] K. Mahajan and J. Gathia, *Child Labour: An Analytical Study* (New Delhi: Centre of Concern for Child Labour, 1992), p. 25. Citing the Indian Council for Child Welfare, Mahajan and Gathia report that "slavery is on the increase among children below the age of 15 years." Gathia also notes, in another study, that the number of children in India who will not be in school by 2000 may be as high as 144 million, indicating there may be tens of millions more child laborers in India by 2000. (See: Child Labour Action Network (CLAN), *Political Campaign for Compulsory Primary Education* (New Delhi: Child Labour Action Network, 1996), p. 2.

[21] Commission on Labour Standards and International Trade, *Child Labour in India: A Perspective*, June 10, 1995, p. 32.

[22] In 1984, the Operations Research Group-Baroda, an independent research organization based in Baroda and Madras, estimated there were forty-four million child laborers in India. Taking into account population growth and employment trends, that figure would be approximately sixty million in 1995. Another frequently cited figure is one hundred million child laborers, a number that corresponds to the government's estimate of all non-school-going children, who are assumed to be working more than eight hours a day. Peace Trust and Bhagwati Environment Development Institute, *From the South*, vol. 2, no. 1, January-March 1995, p. 1. Anti-Slavery International confirmed this estimate of 115 million in a telephone interview on August 14, 1996. Official government figures on the working child population, on the other hand, are based on the 1981 census and are absurdly inaccurate, with the government claiming there are only about seventeen million child laborers. (See chapter on the role of the Indian government.) A 1994 report by the Indian government's Department of Women and Child Development, the Indian Council for Child Welfare, and UNICEF-India concluded that "the number of working children is closer to 90 million than the figure of 20 million assumed by the government." Department of Women and Child Development, Indian Council for Child Welfare, and UNICEF, India Country Office, "Rights of the Child: Report of a National Consultation," November 21-23, 1994.

including a large but uncounted number of girls working as domestic servants. About eleven to eighteen million working children are street children,[23] some of whom are self-employed as shoeshine boys or newspaper vendors, railway porters and ragpickers. Others are forced laborers, working as prostitutes, beggars, drug sellers and petty criminals.[24]

While both boys and girls work as child laborers, the girl child is often subject to even more dismal treatment than her brothers. Girls consistently earn less money than boys (as women earn significantly less than men in India), and are subject to gender-specific forms of abuse from their employers, including rape. In addition to lower pay and greater abuse, girls suffer from the higher demands placed on them within the Indian household. Girls have to work in the house—they tend to the other children, they clean, they go to market, they cook—even if they are also working long and grueling hours outside the home.[25] Furthermore, girls are over represented in some of the most brutal industries to employ child labor. There are twice as many girls as boys laboring in India's quarries and factories, and the majority of children working in the construction industry are girls.[26]

---

[23] There are no accurate statistics that give the number of street children in India. In 1983, the Operations Research Group stated that there were forty-four million working children in India of which eleven million were street children. This number must be considered significantly low, given the fact that the study is now thirteen years old. The government of India's 1991 Census estimated that eighteen million children live and work in India's urban slums (huts, tenements, pavement dwellings), which by the nature of their residence and the fact that they were considered working, qualified them as street children. The estimated population of India's street children is between eleven to eighteen million, based on the Operations Research Group's 1983 estimate and the 1991 Census estimate.

[24] Peace Trust and Bhagwati Environment Development Institute, *From the South*, Vo. 2, No. 1, January-March 1995, p. 1.

[25] At a non-formal education center run during the evenings (as are most, to accommodate the work schedules of the children), Human Rights Watch asked one group of working children what they did for fun. The boys perked up and rattled off a variety of activities: playing with friends, going to the movies, riding a bicycle. The girls, however, were puzzled by the question. Finally a teacher stepped in to explain: the girls do not have the opportunity to do anything for fun; when they are not working for wages or against a loan, they are working for the family.

[26] Mahajan and Gathia, *Child Labour...*, September, 1992, p. 24.

## OVERVIEW OF BONDED CHILD LABOR

Approximately fifteen million children work as bonded laborers in India. Most were put into bondage in exchange for comparatively small sums of money: two thousand rupees—equal to about thirty-five U.S. dollars—is the average amount "loaned" in exchange for a child's labor. To India's vast numbers of extremely poor, however, this money can be, literally, a life-saver. With scant alternative sources of credit available—few rural banks, cooperative credit schemes or government loans—the poor are forced to turn to the local moneylender, who extracts the only collateral available: the promise of their labor or the labor of their children.

Two players create the debt bondage arrangement: the creditor-employer, who offers money to an impoverished parent in an attempt to secure the extremely cheap and captive labor of his or her child, and the parent who accepts this money, agreeing to offer the child's labor as surety for the debt. The child is a commodity of exchange. She or he is powerless to affect the agreement or its terms and—whether willing or unwilling to serve the bond master—powerless to refuse.

The arrangements between parents and contracting agents are usually informal and unwritten. The number of years required to pay off such a loan is indeterminate. Many of the children interviewed by Human Rights Watch had already been working for several years, and even among those relatively new to their jobs, none said that they expected to be released prior to maturity. Some intended to walk away from their bondage when they married, leaving a younger sibling to take over the labor-payment or a parent to somehow extinguish the debt—perhaps by a new loan from a different creditor-employer.

In many industries marked by the use of debt bondage, the child's labor does not function to pay off the original loan at all. Instead, the child's labor serves as both interest on the loan—for the children are paid only a fraction of what their labor would bring them on the open market—and as a surety for the loan's repayment. The original amount loaned to the parent must be repaid in full in a single installment; only then will the child be released from servitude.

The making of beedi cigarettes is one such industry. The average advance in the beedi industry is 1,500 rupees.[27] The average number of beedies a bonded child laborer rolls in a day is 1,500, for an average daily wage of nine rupees. Were the value of the child's labor to be counted as gradual payment of the money

---

[27] Human Rights Watch interview with social activist, November 21, 1995, Madras, Tamil Nadu. Advances in the beedi industry of Tamil Nadu range from 500 to 5,000 rupees. These figures were confirmed by Human Rights Watch interviews with dozens of bonded child beedi rollers.

advanced—and were it calculated honestly, at the official minimum wage established for beedi rolling (30.9 rupees per thousand beedies)—the agent-employer would recoup in labor value the original debt in about six weeks. But the beedi worker's debt is not set off against the value of the labor, and the labor's value is not compensated honestly. If it were, the child would be earning forty to fifty rupees a day instead of nine, and would be able to save enough to quickly fulfill the lump-sum payment requirement of the original advance. As it is, this requirement, together with the abysmally low "wages" paid, virtually ensure that the bonded child will not escape servitude. Most children work many years for their agents, for which the agents, and particularly the owners of the beedi companies, profit handsomely. It is, simply, a severe form of economic exploitation.

Industries that do allow for gradual repayment of the original debt do not provide an easier escape from bondage. First, employers may increase the principal of the loan by adding on to it miscellaneous costs and expenses—the cost of materials, the loss of "defective" goods, meals given to the children, or medical care, on the rare occasions that it is provided. Second, the low wages paid may spur the child's parent to seek an additional loan from the employer. Finally, and most significantly, the value of the child's labor as against the loan is decided by the employer. The bonded children and their parents have virtually no bargaining power with the bond master, with the result that interest rates of 1,200 percent a year, taken out in labor value, are not uncommon.

Regardless of which of these debt structures the child labors under, the end result is the same: it is very difficult to escape bondage. The underlying reason for this difficulty is the grossly unequal power relationships between the child workers and their parents on the one hand and the creditors-cum-employers on the others. The former are frequently low caste, illiterate, and extremely poor. The latter are usually higher caste, literate, comparatively wealthy, and powerful members of the community. Often, these creditors-employers are the only money lenders in town, and as such are extremely influential. They are also frequently connected, by caste and by the social and political hierarchy of the community, with local officials, including police officers, factory inspectors, and other local authorities who might normally be expected to safeguard the rights of children.

Although the exact circumstances of work vary from industry to industry, the hours tend to be long, the pay nominal, and the conditions abysmal. In some industries, children work twelve or more hours a day, seven days a week, receiving only two holidays a year. During their first few years of work they may receive no wages at all, or infrequent pocket change known as "incentives." They are required to work constantly and at a rapid pace; if they work slowly, talk to another child, or make a mistake in their work they will be severely scolded and possibly beaten by their employer, and pay may be deducted from their wages.

Work conditions are dangerous to the health of the child. In the beedi industry, the long hours spent hunched over the basket of tobacco causes growth deformities, and the constant proximity to tobacco dust causes and exacerbates lung diseases; there is a very high rate of tuberculosis in communities dedicated to the manufacture of beedi. In carpet weaving the occupational diseases are similar: the children sit in a cramped space all day long, inhaling wool fibers and dust. As a result, the carpet weavers are prone to emphysema and tuberculosis; they also suffer frequent cuts to their hands and fingers, which may be "cured" by cauterizing them with burning sulphur. Silk workers face similar long and short-term hazards.

The silver workers suffer frequent burns on their hands and arms, the leather workers exposed to toxic chemicals long banned in developed countries, and the gemstone polishers are subject to both cuts and toxic contamination. All of these workers, given their cramped and unsanitary work places, suffer a high risk of contracting tuberculosis and other diseases of poverty.

Three of the industries studied in this report—carpet weaving, beedi rolling, and cloth (silk) weaving—have been classified as "hazardous" under India's Child Labour (Prohibition and Regulation) Act of 1986. Employment of children under fourteen years of age is illegal in these industries. Despite this prohibition, children continue to form the backbone of all three industries, which together employ approximately 850,000 children.[28] Not only has the government failed to enforce this protective legislation, but the government itself is guilty of violating it—the central government's Handloom and Handicrafts Export Corporation runs approximately two hundred "training centers" for child laborers in the carpet industry.[29]

---

[28] There are an estimated 327,000 child workers in the beedi industry (Burra, *Born to Work* p. xxiv); 300,000 child carpet weavers (Mehta., "Cashing in on Child Labor..."); and more than 200,000 children working in silk weaving (see chapter on silk for details and citations).

[29] According to a 1991 study of child labor in India, these training centers include "many [children] well below age fourteen." The manager of one government program claimed that a ban on child labor in the carpet industry would be "suicidal" for exports. See Myron Weiner, *The Child and the State in India* (New Delhi: Oxford University Press, 1991), p. 86

## FACTORS BEHIND BONDED CHILD LABOR:
## POVERTY AND TRADITION

> *A significant use of forced labour has marked the entire spectrum of production in India at all historical periods.*[30]

Slavery in India dates back at least 1,500 years.[31]  Various forms of debt bondage coexisted with formal slavery, and while the British abolished slavery legislatively through the Anti-Slavery Act of 1843, large numbers of former slaves traded their status for that of perpetually bonded servitude.  This was in part due to the fact that the British did not abolish debt-bondage; instead they regulated it. The Workman's Breach of Contract Act, 1859 (13 of 1859) enforced the obligation to provide labor in lieu of an advance, and Section 200 of the Civil Procedure Code, also enacted in 1859, allowed landlords and moneylenders to seize the property of bonded laborers and provided for imprisonment of bonded laborers who did not honor their obligations when they received advances.  The Workman's Breach of Contract Act was repealed in 1925, and Section 200 of the Civil Procedure Code was amended in 1879 to remove punishments for bonded laborers.[32]

The difference between slavery and debt bondage is often rather small, particularly in the context of agriculture.  In both systems workers may be considered to be attached to the land, with ownership of them transferred as part of land sales or exchanges.  Both slavery and debt bondage grant significant powers of ownership to the master:  the worker cannot seek employment elsewhere, the worker cannot refuse to work, the worker is subject to the master's demands twenty-four hours a day, and the master controls the worker's family.  A worker who resists this is subject to severe mistreatment, including beatings and torture.

Many grass-roots organizations, including children's advocates and low-caste and tribal groups, oppose the practice of bonded labor and other forms of

---

[30]  Tanika Sarkar, "Bondage in the Colonial Context," Patnaik and Manjari Dingwaney, eds., *Chains of Servitude: Bondage and Slavery in India* (New Delhi: Sangam Books, 1985), p. 97.

[31]  See generally Uma Chakravarti, "Of Dasas and Karmakaras: Servile Labour in Ancient India," *Chains of Servitude . . .*

[32]  Manjari Dingwaney, "Unredeemed Promises: The Law and Servitude," *Chains of Servitude . . . .*, pp. 312-313.

contemporary slavery. Nonetheless, debt bondage is tolerated by large segments of society who accept it as the normal and proper state of affairs.

Those who stand to gain from the abolition of debt bondage, on the other hand, are precisely those who are least likely to be in a position to exert pressure or claim their rights. Bonded laborers are extremely vulnerable to negative repercussions should they attempt to organize or otherwise agitate for enforcement of the law. Even requests for minimal improvements can lead to a violent response from employers. Bonded laborers have been severely beaten after asking for a raise of a few cents a day, or asking the employer to fulfill a promise to give them a few sacks of grain each year, or for other relatively mild "challenges" to the status quo.[33] Scores of children told Human Rights Watch that their master would beat them if they brought up the subject of wages.

More serious challenges to the master's authority may be met with a more violent or even deadly response. During a much-publicized series of events in 1985, in the state of Haryana, protesting quarry workers were beaten by their employers' hired thugs while uniformed police officers looked on. One of the workers was beaten to death and thirty-four others were seriously wounded. Police later took the injured workers from the hospital to the police station, where they were arrested and fingerprinted.[34]

According to a regional activist in the state of Rajasthan, mine owners continue to respond to labor disputes with unchecked brutality. "Murder and mayhem is nothing to these people. If they are challenged, they will kill the

---

[33] For example: "The children were frequently beaten with iron rods . . . and wounded with scissors . . ., if they were slow in work, or if they asked for adequate food, or if they so much as went to the toilet without the owner's permission." Appendix XV, "Reports on Child Labour of Mirzapur," *Law Relating to the Employment of Children* (1985), p. 160. Another report detailed a woman's attempt to rescue her youngest son after his brother died on the job in a carpet-weaving factory; the employer of her son threatened to kill the boy if she attempted to meet him. "Bonded labourers' mothers want to see PM," *Times of India*, August 14, 1995.

[34] Y. R. Haragopal Reddy, *Bonded Labour System in India* (New Delhi: Deep and Deep Publications, 1995), p. 82. Similar incidents took place across India in the mid-1980s. See, e.g., Ajoy Kumar, "From Slavery to Freedom: The Tale of Chattisgarh Bonded Labourers," Indian Social Institute, 1986, p. 8, reporting that bonded agricultural laborers who attended meetings with labor activists were publicly beaten and driven from their homes.

workers and bury the bodies in the quarries."[35]  The same activist told Human Rights Watch that most government officials in the region have ties to the industry, making legal remedies out of the question.

Poverty is inextricably linked to bondage and the combination of poverty and the lack of access to credit is another essential factor behind bonded labor. Hundreds of millions of India's people are extremely poor and live hand-to-mouth. When additional financial needs arise—to compensate for seasonal declines in earnings or crops, to pay for medical expenses, or to pay for wedding or funeral ceremonies—there is no store of resources available, and the money must be borrowed.

There are very few borrowing options for a poor rural Indian. Even if a bank or cooperative society is accessible—and for most they are not—the poor laborer cannot qualify for a loan, having no security or collateral to offer. With no institutionalized credit sources to turn to, the laborer is forced to take loans from other sources, namely, the local moneylender or local employers or landlords. Often, the village moneylender and the village employer are the same person.

Moneylenders charge 20 percent monthly interest or more. Bond masters charge a much higher rate, but it is less visible since it is taken out in labor value. Many laborers fall into debt bondage as a direct result of borrowing from moneylenders:  they borrow the money, are unable to pay it back because of the accelerated interest rate, then find themselves forced to submit to debt bondage—of themselves or of a child—to obtain enough money to repay the original loan.

### "NIMBLE FINGERS," AND OTHER MYTHS OF CHILD LABOR
A number of myths underlie and perpetuate child labor, justifying it on the grounds that the system "benefits" everyone involved: the country, the community, the family, the craft and the child. Children must be trained at the right age or they will never learn a skill; children must be trained in a profession appropriate to their background and class; children are particularly suited for certain kinds of work because of their "nimble" fingers; and child labor is a natural and desirable function of the family unit. These myths have widespread support.

The "nimble fingers" theory is applied to some of the harshest industries employing children, including the carpet, silk, beedi and silver industries. It asserts that children make the best products in these occupations thanks to their nimble fingers which are, according to the myth, better able to tie the tiny knots of wool, unravel thread from boiling silk cocoons, and solder tiny silver flowers to a chain. In this view, child labor is not an evil, but a production necessity.   This

---

[35] Human Rights Watch interview with rural activist, Dec. 13, 1995, Rajasthan.

rationalization is a lie. In fact, children make the cheaper goods; only master weavers make the best quality carpets and saris.

The myth that children must be trained at the "right" age—at six or seven years of age, or younger—contends that children who go to school, postponing their craft training until adolescence, either will be unable to adequately learn a skill or will be at an irreparable disadvantage in comparison with those who did begin working as young children. A study on child labor in Varanasi summarized the calculation behind this logic:

> Any number of justifications are available at the community level in support of children taking up a job at an early age. It is said that in order to learn the craft properly one has to start working away from the family. Further, in order to become an accomplished artisan one has to start working at an early age. Those who start working at the "late" age of 12 years might pick up the craft within a few months but they would never be able to pick up speed in their work. As against this, those starting at the "right" age of six or seven years become very good workers after an apprenticeship of 5 to 6 years. Whatever be the truth behind the general belief, it ensures continuous availability of child labour at low wages.[36]

---

[36] R. K Misra., *Preliminary Report on the Child Labour in the Saree Industry of Varanasi*, Human Rights Cell, Banaras Hindu University, Varanasi, 1995, p. 13.

# IV. LEGAL CONTEXT

## APPLICABLE INTERNATIONAL LAW

The practice of bonded child labor violates the following international human rights conventions; India is a party to all of them, and as such is legally bound to comply with their terms.

### Convention on the Suppression of Slave Trade and Slavery, 1926

This convention requires signatories to "prevent and suppress the slave trade" and "to bring about, progressively and as soon as possible, the complete abolition of slavery in all its forms." It also obligates parties to "take all necessary measures to prevent compulsory or forced labor from developing into conditions analogous to slavery."[37]

### Supplementary Convention on the Abolition of Slavery, the Slave Trade, and Institutions and Practices Similar to Slavery, 1956

The supplementary convention on slavery offers further clarification of prohibited practices and refers specifically to debt bondage and child servitude as institutions similar to slavery. It requires States Parties to "take all practicable and necessary legislative and other measures to bring about progressively and as soon as possible the complete abolition of... debt bondage... [and] any institution or practice whereby a child or young person under the age of 18 years, is delivered by either or both of his natural parents or by his guardian to another person, whether for reward or not, with a view to the exploitation of the child or young person or of his labour."[38] The convention defines debt bondage as follows:

> Debt bondage, that is to say, the status or condition arising from a pledge by a debtor of his personal services or those of a person under his control as security for a debt, if the value of those

---

[37] Convention on the Suppression of Slave Trade and Slavery, signed at Geneva, September 25, 1926; Protocol Amended the Slavery Convention, signed at Geneva, September 25, 1926, with annex, done at, New York, December 7, 1953, entered into force, December 7, 1953. A slave is someone "over whom any or all of the powers attaching to the right of ownership are exercised." Supplementary Convention on the Abolition of Slavery, the Slave Trade, and Institutions and Practices Similar to Slavery, done at Geneva, September 7, 1956; entered into force, April 30, 1957 (Supplementary Convention).

[38] Supplementary Convention on the Abolition of Slavery.

24

services as reasonably assessed is not applied towards the liquidation of the debt or the length and nature of those services are not respectively limited and defined.[39]

### *Forced Labour Convention, 1930*

The International Labour Organisation (ILO) Forced Labour Convention requires signatories to "suppress the use of forced or compulsory labour in all its forms in the shortest period possible."[40] In 1957, the ILO explicitly incorporated debt bondage and serfdom within its definition of forced labor.[41]

### *International Covenant on Civil and Political Rights (ICCPR), 1966*

Article 8 of the ICCPR prohibits slavery and the slave trade in all their forms, servitude, and forced or compulsory labor. Article 24 entitles all children to "the right to such measures of protection as are required by his status as a minor, on the part of his family, society and the State."[42]

### *International Covenant on Economic, Social and Cultural Rights (ICESCR), 1966*

Article 7 of the ICESCR provides that States Parties shall "recognize the right of everyone to the enjoyment of just and favourable conditions of work." Article 10 requires Parties to protect "children and young persons... from economic and social exploitation."[43]

---

[39] Ibid.

[40] Forced Labour Convention (No. 29), 1930, adopted at Geneva, June 28, 1930, as modified by the Final Articles Revision Convention, adopted at Montreal, October 9, 1946.

[41] International Labour Organisation, *Conventions and Recommendations 1919-1966* (Geneva: ILO, 1966), p. 891. The ILO also passed the Abolition of Forced Labour Convention (No. 105) in 1957; India, however, chose not to sign this convention.

[42] International Covenant on Civil and Political Rights, G.A. Res. 2200 (XXI), 21 U.N. GAOR Supp. (No. 16), U.N. Doc. A/6316 (1966) (entered into force March 23, 1976).

[43] International Covenant on Economic, Social and Cultural Rights, G.A. Res. 2200 (XXI), 21 U.N. GAOR Supp. (No. 16), U.N. Doc. A/6316 (entered into force January 3, 1976).

### Convention on the Rights of the Child, 1989

The following three provisions mandate protections that are particularly relevant for the bonded child laborer:

Article 32: "States Parties recognize the right of the child to be protected from economic exploitation and from performing any work that is likely to be hazardous or... be harmful to the child's health or physical, mental, spiritual, moral or social development."[44]   States are directed to implement these protections through appropriate legislative, administrative, social and educational measures.   In particular, they are to:

> (a) provide for a minimum age or minimum ages for admissions to employment;
> (b)   provide for appropriate regulation of the hours and conditions of employment; and
> (c) provide for appropriate penalties or other sanctions to ensure the effective enforcement of this article.[45]

Article 35: "States Parties shall take all appropriate. . . measures to prevent the abduction, the sale of or traffic in children for any purpose or in any form."[46] A significant portion of the bonded child laborers of India are trafficked from one state to another, and some are sold outright.[47]

Article 36: "States Parties shall protect the child against all other forms of exploitation prejudicial to any aspects of the child's welfare."[48]

---

[44] Convention on the Rights of the Child, G.A. Res. 44/125, U.N. GAOR, 44th Session, Supp. No. 49, U.N. Doc. A/44/736 (1989) (entered into force September 2, 1990).

[45] Ibid. India ratified the Convention subject to a reservation that these economic and social rights will be "progressively implemented," "subject to the extent of available resources."

[46] Ibid.

[47] See chapter on carpets; see also Human Rights Watch/Asia, *Rape for Profit: Trafficking of Nepali Girls and Women to India's Brothels* (Human Rights Watch: New York, 1995).

[48] Convention on the Rights of the Child, G.A. Res. 44/125, U.N. GAOR, 44th Session, Supp. No. 49, U.N. Doc. A/44/736 (1989) (entered into force September 2, 1990).

## APPLICABLE DOMESTIC LAW

A plethora of national laws, some dating back to the 1930s, offer protection from exploitation to India's working children. The Bonded Labour System (Abolition) Act of 1976 is, for the purposes of this report, the most significant and far-reaching of these laws—it outlaws all debt bondage, including that of children, and it requires government intervention and rehabilitation of the bonded worker. It is further set apart from the other laws by the fact that it has none of the exemptions from compliance that virtually nullify many of India's other labor laws. Unfortunately, lack of loopholes is no guarantee of enforcement. The Bonded Labour System (Abolition) Act, the Child Labour (Prohibition and Regulation) Act, and the other pieces of protective legislation that apply in varying circumstances to the situation of the bonded child laborer, are betrayed by an extremely low rate of enforcement. This lack of enforcement is discussed in the chapter on the role of the Indian government.

Every industry discussed in this report, and every individual case referred to, violates the Bonded Labour System (Abolition) Act and the constitutional provisions that underlie such an act. These violations represent the most severe and egregious of the many legal failings contributing to the persistence of bonded child labor in India. All of the cases and all of the industries mentioned in this report also violate the Child Labour (Prohibition and Regulation) Act: they all violate its regulatory provisions, and the largest and most significant industries—beedi, carpets, and silk—also violate its prohibitory provisions. In addition to violating these two centerpieces of protective legislation, most industries also violate one or more of the following laws: the Factories Act; the Beedi and Cigar Workers (Conditions of Employment) Act; the Contract Labour (Regulation and Abolition) Act; and the Inter-State Migrant Workmen (Regulation of Employment and Conditions of Service) Act. All cases documented in this report also violate the Children (Pledging of Labour) Act, which is similar in its protections to the Bonded Labour System (Abolition) Act.

In addition, under the Indian Penal Code (IPC) rape, extortion, causing grievous hurt, assault, kidnapping, abduction, wrongful confinement, buying or disposing of people as slaves, and unlawful compulsory labor are criminal offences, punishable with up to ten years imprisonment and fines. Under the Juvenile Justice Act, 1986, cruelty to juveniles and withholding the earnings of a juvenile are criminal offences, punishable with up to three years imprisonment and fines.

## *Indian Constitution*

Article 21 of the Constitution of India guarantees the right to life and liberty. The Indian Supreme Court has interpreted the right of liberty to include, among other things, the right of free movement, the right to eat, sleep and work when one pleases, the right to be free from inhuman and degrading treatment, the right to integrity and dignity of the person, the right to the benefits of protective labor legislation, and the right to speedy justice.[49] The practice of bonded labor violates all of these constitutionally-mandated rights.

Article 23 of the constitution prohibits the practice of debt bondage and other forms of slavery both modern and ancient:

> Traffic in human beings and *begar* and other similar forms of forced labour are prohibited and any contravention of this provision shall be an offence punishable in accordance with the law.

*Begar* is an ancient caste-based obligation, a "form of forced labour under which a person is compelled to work without receiving any remuneration."[50] "Other similar forms of forced labour" was interpreted expansively by the Supreme Court in 1982, when it ruled in the seminal *Asiad Workers' Case* that both unpaid and paid labour were prohibited by Article 23, so long as the element of force or compulsion was present in the worker's ongoing services to the employer. Examples of force include overt physical compulsion and compulsion under threat of legal sanction (as for example in the case of an allegedly unpaid debt), as well as more subtle forms of compulsion, including "compulsion arising from hunger and poverty, want and destitution."[51]

Given the dire economic straits of most Indians, this definition could bring hundreds of millions of people within its scope. The Supreme Court went on, however, to provide a helpful rule for determining exactly what situations

---

[49] See S. K. Singh, *Bonded Labour and the Law* (New Delhi: Deep and Deep Publications, 1994), pp. 48-51.

[50] *People's Union for Democratic Rights v. Union of India [Asiad Workers' Case]*, AIR 1982 S.C. 1473, paragraph 1486.

[51] Ibid., paragraph 1490. For a discussion of Supreme Court decisions affecting bonded labourers, see Y. R. Haragopal Reddy, *Bonded Labour System in India* (New Delhi: Deep and Deep Publications, 1995), ch. 4.

constitute forced labor. "[W]here a person provides labour or service to another for remuneration which is less than minimum wage, the labour or service provided by him clearly falls within the scope and ambit of the word 'forced labour'..."[52] All labor rewarded with less than the minimum wage, then, constitutes forced labor and violates the Constitution of India.

In another landmark case, this one brought on behalf of a group of bonded quarry workers in the early 1980s, the Supreme Court ruled that "[i]t is the plainest requirement of Articles 21 and 23 of the Constitution that bonded labourers must be identified and released and on release, they must be suitably rehabilitated.... [A]ny failure of action on the part of the State Government[s] in implementing the provisions of [the Bonded Labour System (Abolition) Act] would be the clearest violation of Article 21 [and] Article 23 of the Constitution."[53]

Article 24 prohibits the employment of children in factories, mines, and other hazardous occupations.[54] Together, Articles 23 and 24 are placed under the heading "Right against Exploitation," one of India's constitutionally-proclaimed fundamental rights.

Article 39 requires the state to "direct its policy toward securing":

> (e) that the health and strength of workers... and the tender age of children are not abused and that citizens are not forced by economic necessity to enter avocations unsuited to their age or strength.
> (f) that children are given opportunities and facilities to develop in a healthy manner and in conditions of freedom and dignity and that childhood and youth are protected against exploitation and against moral and material abandonment."

---

[52] *People's Union for Democratic Rights* v. *Union of India*, (1982) 3 SCC 235, paragraphs 259-260.

[53] *Neeraja Chaudhary* v. *State of Madhya Pradesh*, 3 SCC 243, paragraph 255 (1984).

[54] "No child below the age of fourteen years shall be employed to work in any factory or mine or engaged in any other hazardous employment." Constitution of India, Article 24.

## Bonded Labour System (Abolition) Act, 1976

The Bonded Labour System (Abolition) Act purports to abolish all debt agreements and obligations arising out of India's longstanding bonded labor system. It is the legislative fulfillment of the Indian Constitution's mandate against *begar* and forced labor.[55] It frees all bonded laborers, cancels any outstanding debts against them, prohibits the creation of new bondage agreements, and orders the economic rehabilitation of freed bonded laborers by the state.[56] It also criminalizes all post-act attempts to compel a person to engage in bonded labor, with maximum penalties of three years in prison and a 2,000 rupee fine.[57] The Bonded Labour System (Abolition) Act offers the following definition of the practices being abolished.

> Sec. 2(g) "bonded labour system" means the system of forced, or partly forced labour under which a debtor enters...or is presumed to have entered, into an agreement with the creditor to the effect that,—
>
> (i) in consideration of an advance obtained by him or by any of his lineal ascendants or descendants (whether or not such advance is evidenced by any document) and in consideration of the interest, if any, due on such advance, or
>
> (ii) in pursuance of any customary or social obligation, or
>
> (iii) in pursuance of an obligation devolving on him by succession, or
>
> (iv) for any economic consideration received by him or by any of his lineal ascendants or descendants, or

---

[55] Consequently, post-act social action litigation on behalf of bonded laborers is brought under both the Bonded Labour System (Abolition) Act and the Constitution of India. For a discussion of cases see Reddy, *Bonded Labour System in India*, ch. 4.

[56] The Bonded Labour System (Abolition) Act, 1976, Sec. 4, 5, 6, and 14. See Appendix for full text.

[57] Ibid., Sec. 16. The maximum penalties for a first-time offender under the Child Labour (Prohibition and Regulation) Act are weaker than the Bonded Labour System (Abolition) Act in terms of potential length of incarceration (one year), but significantly stronger in terms of monetary punishment (ten to twenty thousand rupees). See the Child Labour (Prohibition and Regulation) Act, Sec. 14 (1).

(v) by reason of his birth in any particular caste or community, he would—

(1) render, by himself or through any member of his family... labour or service to the creditor, or for the benefit of the creditor, for a specified period or for an unspecified period, either without wages or for nominal wages, or

(2) forfeit the freedom of employment or other means of livelihood for a specified period or for an unspecified period, or

(3) forfeit the right to move freely throughout the territory of India, or

(4) forfeit the right to appropriate or sell at market value any of his property or product of his labour or the labour of a member of his family or any person dependent on him...

This definition is meant to, and does, cover all of the many permutations of the bonded labor system in modern India. There are differences from one part of the country to the next and from one industry or landlord to another in terms of wages paid, the amount advanced, whether the advance is considered a type of loan or a type of wage, the hours worked per day and days worked per year, and whether the worker has some freedom from the bond master or is kept under constant control. Some bonded laborers receive no wages at all, apart from meager food stipends and a yearly change of clothing; some receive extremely low wages, constituting as little as 10 percent of the mandated minimum wage; some receive a standard wage in theory, but in fact lose 70 or 80 percent of it, sight unseen, back to the employer as "interest" on the advance. Some laborers are working to pay off a 500 rupee loan, others a 15,000 rupee loan. Some inherited their debt from their parents; others have contracted for a ten-month period of servitude. Some work sixteen hours a day, 365 days a year, every year of their lives. Others work ten hours a day, six days a week. Despite these differences, all are bonded laborers within the definition of the act.

It is what they have in common that determines their bonded status: they are working for nominal wages in consideration of an advance, and they are not free to discontinue their work. These three elements—an advance, low wages, and compulsion—are at the core of all bonded labor. The act defines "nominal wages" as those that are less than minimum wages or, where no minimum wage has been set, less than wages normally paid for the same or similar work in the same locality.[58]

District magistrates—called district collectors, or deputy commissioners, in some states—are responsible for enforcement of the Bonded Labour System (Abolition) Act.[59] The district magistrate, an appointed civil servant, is the top authority at the district level and as such oversees government administration, including the administration of justice. His duties are varied and many, and include overseeing the work of fifty to sixty distinct departments.[60] In addition to these duties, he is required by the Bonded Labour System (Abolition) Act to identify all cases of bonded labor occurring in his district, free the laborers, and initiate prosecution under the act. He is also charged with making sure available credit sources are in place, so that freed laborers will not be forced into bondage again.[61] Finally, the district magistrate is to constitute and participate in the functioning of

---

[58] Ibid., Sec. 2(1)(I)(a) and (b). Because no minimum wages have been set by the government for children's work, the second prong of this definition applies. See also *People's Union for Democratic Rights* v. *Union of India*, (1982) 3 SCC 235, paragraphs 259-260, in which the Supreme Court ruled that "where a person provides labour or service to another for remuneration which is less than minimum wage, the labour or service provided by him clearly falls within the scope and ambit of the word 'forced labour'..." All forms of forced labor are forbidden under the Bonded Labour System (Abolition) Act.

[59] "It shall be the duty of every District Magistrate and every officer specified by him under Sec. 10 to inquire whether after the commencement of this act, any bonded labour system or any other form of forced labour is being enforced by, or on behalf of, any person resident within the local limits of his jurisdiction and if, as a result of such inquiry, any person is found to be enforcing the bonded labour system or any other system of forced labour, he shall forthwith take such action as may be necessary to eradicate the enforcement of such forced labour." Bonded Labour System (Abolition) Act, 1976, Sec. 12.

[60] Human Rights Watch interview with Mirzapur District Collector Mr. Bachittar Singh, December 19, 1995, Mirzapur. A 1994 study describing the multifarious duties of district magistrates notes that "[n]o district magistrate can properly perform all the assignments given to him." See also S. K. Singh, *Bonded Labour and the Law*, p. 124-125, 142, 147.

[61] Ibid., Sec. 11 requires the district magistrate to "as far as practicable, try to promote the welfare of the freed bonded labourer by securing and protecting the economic interest of such bonded labourer so that he may not have any occasion or reason to contract any further bonded debt."

a district-level "vigilance committee." The statutory functions of this committee are:

> (a) to advise the District Magistrate . . . . as to the efforts made, and action taken, to ensure that the provisions of this act... are properly implemented;
> (b) to provide for the economic and social rehabilitation of the freed bonded labourers;
> (c) to coordinate the functions of rural banks and cooperative societies with a view to canalizing adequate credit to the freed bonded labourers;
> (d) to keep an eye on the number of offences of which cognizance has been taken under [the] act;
> (e) to make a survey as to whether there is any offence of which cognizance ought to be taken under the act;
> (f) to defend any suit instituted against a freed bonded labourer or a member of his family... for the recovery of the whole or part of any bonded debt...[62]

Very few such vigilance committees have been formed, and Human Rights Watch knows of no district in which such a committee is currently operative.

References to rehabilitation of freed bonded laborers occur twice in the Bonded Labour System (Abolition) Act—once in reference to the district magistrate's duty to "secure and protect the economic interests" of the bonded laborer (Sec. 11), and once in stipulating the vigilance committees' duty to provide for the "economic and social rehabilitation" of the bonded laborer (Sec. 14). The act itself, however, does not specify of what this rehabilitation should consist and left implementation of rehabilitation up to the state governments, and largely dependent on the initiative of District Magistrates.

In 1978, the Ministry of Labour launched a scheme that specified a "rehabilitation allowance" in order to assist state governments with rehabilitation.[63] Under this scheme, the central government contributes half of the rehabilitation assistance allowance due to every freed bonded laborer, and the state where the bonded laborer resides pays the other half. The allowance, determined by a Ministry of Labour Planning Commission, was originally set at 4,000 rupees. It

---

[62] Ibid., Sec. 14.

[63] Reddy, *Bonded Labour System in India*, p. 163.

has been raised once, to 6,250 rupees, in 1986.[64] In 1982, cognizant of the reasons that lead to bondage and possibility of relapse if those released are not rehabilitated, the government expanded this program by adding guidelines for rehabilitation under Ministry of Labor Direct Order No. S.11011/20/82-BL, which stated that:

> (i) Psychological rehabilitation must go side by side with physical and economic rehabilitation;
> (ii) The physical and economic rehabilitation has fifteen major components namely allotment of house-sites and agricultural land, land development, provision of low cost dwelling units, agriculture, provision of credit, horticulture, animal husbandry, training for acquiring new skills and develop in existing skills, promoting traditional arts and crafts, provision of wages employment and enforcement of minimum wages, collection and processing of minor forest products, health, medical care and sanitation, supply of essential commodities, education of children of bonded labourers and protection of civil rights;
> (iii) There is scope for bringing about an integration among the various Central and Centrally Sponsored Schemes and the ongoing schemes of State Government for more qualitative rehabilitation. The essence of such duplication, i.e., pooling resources from different sources for the same purpose. It should be ensured that while funds are not drawn from different sources for the same purpose, [funds] drawn from different sectors [schemes] for different components of the rehabilitation scheme are integrated skillfully; and
> (iv) While drawing up any scheme/programme of rehabilitation of freed bonded labour, the latter must necessarily be given the choice between the various alternatives for their rehabilitation and such programme should be finally selected for execution as would need the total requirements of the families of freed bonded laborers to enable them to cross the poverty line on the

---

[64] Ibid., citing, *inter alia*, Lr. No. Y-11011/4/84-BL, dated February 14, 1986, Director General (Labour Welfare), Ministry of Labour, Government of India.

one hand and to prevent them from sliding back into debt bondage on the other.[65]

In its *1994-95 Annual Report,* the Ministry of Labour stated that funds for rehabilitation assistance would be increased from Rs. 6,250 to Rs.10,000 for each bonded laborer, and that "respective State Governments will undertake further surveys to identify bonded labourers as may still be in existence and report to the Government of India. The State Governments have also agreed to undertake selective follow-up studies to assess whether rehabilitated bonded labourers have relapsed into bondage and to set up Vigilance Committees, wherever they are not in existence."[66]

However, the extent to which bonded laborers have been identified, released, and rehabilitated by government officials has been negligible; this is discussed in the chapter on the role of the government.

### Children (Pledging of Labour) Act, 1933

This act predates Independence but remains in force. It is rarely used and rarely mentioned in discussions of bonded labor and child labor, probably because the more recent laws carry penalties that, while lenient themselves, are nonetheless stiffer than those of the Children (Pledging of Labour) Act.

The act calls for penalties to be levied against any parent, middleman, or employer involved in making or executing a pledge of a child's labor. Such a pledge is defined as an "agreement, written or oral, express or implied, whereby the parent or guardian of a child, in return for any payment or benefit received or to be received by him, undertakes to cause or allow the services of the child to be utilized in any employment."[67] Lawful labor agreements are limited to those made in consideration of reasonable wages and terminable at seven days' or less notice. The fines for violating this law are fifty rupees against the parent and two hundred rupees against either the middleman or employer.[68]

---

[65] Ibid., p.166.

[66] Ministry of Labour, *Annual Report 1994-1995*, p.97.

[67] The Children (Pledging of Labour) Act, 1933, Sec. 2. "Child" is a person less than fifteen years old.

[68] Ibid., Sec. 4 - 6.

## Child Labour (Prohibition and Regulation) Act, 1986

The Child Labour (Prohibition and Regulation) Act was enacted in 1986 and defines a child as "a person who has not completed their fourteenth year of age."[69] It does not prohibit child labor *per se*, nor does it set a minimum age for the employment of children. Instead, it regulates the hours and conditions of work for child laborers, while prohibiting the employment of children in twenty-five hazardous industries.[70] Three of the enumerated hazardous industries rely heavily on bonded labor and were included in the Human Rights Watch investigation. These three industries are the beedi (hand-rolled indigenous cigarettes) industry, carpet-weaving, and cloth printing, dyeing and weaving. The other industries discussed in this report are subject to the regulatory aspects of the Child Labour (Prohibition and Regulation) Act. However, implementation of the regulatory provisions of the act require each state to formulate an act-specific set of rules and regulations; the majority of states have not done so as of 1996, ten years after passage of the act.

For first convictions under the hazardous industries prohibition, the act prescribes imprisonment of three to twelve months or a fine of 10,000 to 20,000 rupees. Second offenses are to be punished with a mandatory six months to two years in prison. There are no standing requirements for the filing of a complaint under the Child Labor Act. Any person, including but not limited to any police officer or government inspector, is authorized to file a complaint before any court of competent jurisdiction.

---

[69] Child Labour (Prohibition and Regulation) Act, 1986, Part I, Section 2(ii).

[70] The twenty-five occupations and industries where child labor is prohibited are: beedi-making; carpet-weaving; cement manufacture; cloth printing, dyeing and weaving; manufacture of matches, explosives and fireworks; mica-cutting and splitting; shellac manufacture; soap manufacture; tanning; wool-cleaning; the building and construction industry; manufacture of slate pencils; manufacture of agate products; manufacturing processes using toxic metals and substances; "hazardous processes" as defined by the Factories Act, Sec. 87; printing as defined by the Factories Act, Sec. 2; cashew and cashewnut processing; soldering processes in electronic industries, railway transportation; cinder picking, ashpit clearing or building operations in railway premises; vending operations at railway stations; work on ports; sale of firecracker and fireworks; and work in slaughter houses. Child Labour (Prohibition and Regulation) Act, 1986, Part II (Prohibition of employment of children in certain occupations and processes), Sec. 3, Schedules A and B; as amended by Government Notification Nos. No.SO 404(E) (June 5, 1989) and No. SO. 263(E) (March 29, 1994).

The act also authorizes central and state governments to appoint inspectors charged with securing compliance with the act. Rather than do this, most states have added responsibility for enforcement of the Child Labour (Prohibition and Regulation) Act on to the already-existing ranks of the labor inspectors. This is an undesirable arrangement for two reasons. First, requiring the labor inspectors to also investigate violations of the Child Labour (Prohibition and Regulation) Act saddles them with an unrealistic work burden. Even before the 1986 Child Labour (Prohibition and Regulation) Act was added to their responsibilities, a 1979 report by a government-appointed Committee on Child Labour found the inspectors overwhelmed by their duties:

> The jurisdiction of individual inspectors was too extensive for them to keep a regular watch on activities within their purview. In several States one inspector was required to cover a group of several districts. He was also burdened with very wide ranging other responsibilities pertaining to labour legislation. [As a result of] this situation...there were practically no prosecutions... of any violation of existing laws pertaining to child labour.[71]

In practice, some labor inspectors enforce the Factories Act while others enforce the Child Labour (Prohibition and Regulation) Act, a not very efficient division of labor.[72] Furthermore, a 1995 government-mandated report on child labor found that "many inspectors were unclear about the import of laws."[73]

In addition to being overextended, factory and labor inspectors in India are notoriously corrupt and susceptible to bribery.[74] Against this background, there

---

[71] Myron Weiner, *The Child and the State in India* (New Delhi: Oxford University Press, 1991), pp. 80-81.

[72] Commission on Labour Standards and International Trade, *Child Labour in India...*, p. 40.

[73] Ibid.

[74] The prevalence of corruption among factory and labor inspectors and other charged with enforcing child labor laws was confirmed to Human Rights Watch by multiple sources, including an official of the national government. See also Commission on Labour Standards, *Child Labour in India...* , p. 40.

is little reason to expect them to vigorously find and root out instances of illegal child labor.

Even if inspection were reliable, glaring loopholes in the Child Labour (Prohibition and Regulation) Act allow manufacturers to escape application of the law quite easily. First, the Child Labour (Prohibition and Regulation) Act applies to all workshops which make use of child labor in prohibited processes, *except* those workshops "wherein any process is carried on by the occupier with the aid of his family..."[75] The vast majority of child labor takes place in agriculture and cottage industries in the informal sector. Often, the employer does have one of his own children or a niece or nephew working alongside the rest of the children, and this is enough to take his shop out of the purview of the Child Labour (Prohibition and Regulation) Act. Even if he does not have a family member working on the premises, he is likely to say that he does, according to labor inspectors, social welfare activists and others familiar with the informal sector.

This exception gives tacit government approval to the use of child labor, when the child is a relative of the family, under conditions that would otherwise be illegal. This exception includes the use of a child labor in hazardous occupations or industries. Nor is this the only exception to the application of the Child Labour (Prohibition and Regulation) Act. The act is also inapplicable to government-sponsored schools or training programs. Again, this means that work and conditions ordinarily deemed harmful to children are considered *non-harmful* so long as they take place under the auspices of an official government program. The best examples of this exception are the approximately two hundred government-run carpet weaving training centers.[76] Carpet weaving is a hazardous and therefore prohibited industry under the Child Labour (Prohibition and Regulation) Act. Under the exception for government schools, however, thousands of children are enrolled in this industry, not only with government approval, but with government facilitation and encouragement.

These exceptions are clear violations Article 24 of the Indian Constitution, which states that "no child below 14 shall be employed in any factory or mine or engaged in any hazardous employment."

Another major loophole in the Child Labour (Prohibition and Regulation) Act concerns the proof of age of the child worker. One would expect the employer to carry the burden of proof that the working child is of legal age. This is not the case. Instead, the Child Labour (Prohibition and Regulation) Act effectively puts

---

[75] The Child Labour (Prohibition and Regulation) Act, 1986, Sec. 3.

[76] See chapter on handwoven carpets.

the onus of proof on the state, stipulating that, in the event of a dispute between the employer and the government inspector as to the age of the working child, "the question shall... be referred by the Inspector for decision to the prescribed medical authority."[77] What this means in practice is that on those rare occasions when labor inspectors do pay a visit to production sites, they must pay a doctor to accompany them and evaluate the age of the children. Even then the truth of the matter of age is not necessarily settled, as manufacturers are known to bribe the medical authorities—not to mention the inspectors themselves—in order to obtain favorable results.[78]

These loopholes create daunting enforcement difficulties in the beedi, carpet, and silk industries—the three industries that are both heavily bonded and where child labor of any sort is outlawed by the Child Labour (Prohibition and Regulation) Act. The same difficulties would be noted in the other prohibited industries of the act.

Every industry studied by Human Rights Watch thoroughly violates the protective regulations of the Child Labour (Prohibition and Regulation) Act. These violated provisions include the right to an hour of rest after three hours of work; a maximum work day of six hours; a prohibition of child work before 8:00 a.m. or after 7:00 p.m.; a prohibition on overtime; a mandatory day of rest every week; and the requirement that various health and safety precautions be observed.

### Factories Act, 1948

The Factories Act strictly forbids the employment of children less than fourteen years old in factories.[79] It also includes a sizable loophole, in that the act only applies to factories employing ten or more people with the use of electric or other forms of generated power, or twenty or more people without the use of

---

[77] Ibid., Sec. 10.

[78] According to R. V. Pillai, the Secretary General of the National Human Rights Commission (NHRC), there is frequent collusion between medical officers of the government and employers of child labor, who bribe the medical officers in order to obtain certificates stating the children working for them are above the age of fourteen. Secretary General Pillai stated that some medical officers are "notorious" for engaging in these acts, to the extent that the NHRC has recommended to some district magistrates that they file criminal charges against corrupt medical officers. Human Rights Watch interview with Secretary General Pillai, December 28, 1995, New Delhi.

[79] "No child who has not completed his fourteenth year shall be required or allowed to work in any factory." The Factories Act, 1948, Sec. 67.

power.[80]   Many small scale industries intentionally fragment the manufacturing process into separate units in order to circumvent application of the Factories Act.[81] Others only employ small numbers of people on the books, bringing in dozens of others as unofficial "extras."[82]

### Beedi and Cigar Workers (Conditions of Employment) Act, 1966
See chapter on beedi cigarettes.

### Scheduled Castes/Scheduled Tribes Prevention of Atrocities Act, 1989
This act defines any kind of forced labor, including bonded labor, as an "atrocity" if the victim is a member of a scheduled caste or tribe.  Committing an "atrocity" is punishable with up to five years imprisonment and fine.[83]

### Inter-State Migrant Workmen (Regulation of Employment and Conditions of Service) Act, 1979
This law regulates the employment of inter-state workers migrant workers. It requires that establishments employing such workers be registered, that contractors be licensed and keep records of all migrant workers recruited, that migrant workers be paid at the same rate as non-migrant workers, and that inspections be carried out to ensure compliance with these provisions.[84]

---

[80]   Ibid., Sec. 2(m)(I) and (ii).

[81]   To get around this restriction, factory owners have been known to "partition their premises and isolate the areas where work is being done with power." See Burra, *Born to Work*, p. 75.

[82]   According to Burra: "In order to evade the Factories Act, ninety per cent of the units show that they have less than nine workers.  In some factories I visited, I noticed around fifty workers.  But when I asked the employer, he said there were only eight people working there!" Ibid., p. 136.

[83]   The Scheduled Castes and The Scheduled Tribes (Prevention of Atrocities) Act, 1989, Section 3(1).

[84]   The Inter-State Migrant Workmen (Regulation of Employment and Conditions of Service) Act, 1979, ch. II - ch. VI.

### Contract Labour (Regulation and Abolition) Act, 1970

This act regulates the use of contract labor and provides for its abolition in certain industries, at the discretion of the appropriate government (state or central ). Among its provisions are a requirement that no wage period exceed one month.[85]

### Minimum Wages Act, 1948

The Minimum Wages Act sets the minimum wage for certain enumerated occupations and requires that overtime be paid to all workers who work beyond a "normal working day." In the case of children under fourteen, a "normal working day" is four and a half hours.

### Plantation Labour Act, 1951

This act regulates the work and wage conditions of plantation workers, including children over the age of fourteen.

### Apprentices Act, 1961

The Apprentices Act regulates the rights and work hours of apprentices, and sets the minimum age for apprenticeships at fourteen years.

### Shops and Establishments Act, 1961

This law, which applies to shops, hotels, restaurants, and places of amusement, regulates the hours of work and prohibits the employment of children below a certain age, to be determined by the states. In eleven states, the minimum age for a child worker is fourteen years; in thirteen states, the minimum age is twelve years.[86]

---

[85] The Contract Labour (Regulation and Abolition) Act, 1970, Sec. 6, 10, and 64.

[86] Campaign Against Child Labour (CACL), "Reference Kit on Child Labour for Media Persons," January 1995.

Beedi rollers, the adult on the left bought himself out of bondage several years ago and the boy on the right was recently released under the District Collector's scheme, Vellore, Tamil Nadu.

Bonded silver workers, Salem, Tamil Nadu.

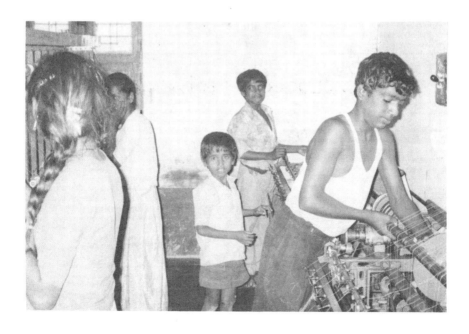

Above and Below: Bonded children involved in silk reeling and twisting, Magadi, Karnataka.

Above and Below: Bonded children involved in the weaving of silk saris in Kanchipuram, Tamil Nadu.

Bonded shoemaker, involved in cutting wooden heels for shoes, Bombay, Maharashtra.

Girls bonded as agricultural laborers, Anekal Taluk, Karnataka.

## V. CHILDREN IN BONDAGE

**BEEDI**

Sumathi, a twelve-year-old girl, is the oldest sibling of five; three of the five are girls, and the three sisters all roll beedi. The youngest, eight years old, works at home as a tip closer. The second, nine years old, was bonded to an agent three years ago for an advance of 1,000 rupees; she works full time as a tip closer, earning only three rupees a week.

Sumathi herself was bonded when she was seven in exchange for a 1,000 rupee advance. She rolls 1,500 beedies a day, for which she earns five rupees. She told Human Rights Watch:

> My father and mother force me to go to work with the agent. The agent often beats me. If I tell my father, he allows me to stay home the following day, but then they are pushing me to go again. My father and mother say I have to go. I don't want to go. I am afraid of my agent. But my parents force me to go, if I don't go they scold me and beat me.

> Every week the agent gives my wages to my parents. If it is less money than usual, they beat me.

> In my family there are seven members, so it is difficult to even get enough food to eat. That's why my father goes to the agent—to ask for more money. But the agent won't give it, because he says I don't work hard enough. But every day I am being sent back to the agent.[87]

*******

"Beedi" is a domestically-produced and consumed Indian cigarette. Though cheaper than manufactured filter-tip cigarettes, it is a relatively expensive product—a pack of twenty-four beedies costs between ten and twenty rupees—and one that is heavily consumed, with more than 500 billion beedi cigarettes produced

---

[87] All testimonies in this report are from children interviewed by Human Rights Watch researchers in November and December, 1995, except where otherwise noted. All names have been changed.

46

and smoked each year.[88]  With annual sales worth forty billion rupees, beedi is one of India's most significant domestic products.[89]

More than 325,000 children labor in the beedi industry, most in the southern state of Tamil Nadu.[90]  Other states with beedi production are Madhya Pradesh, Maharashtra, West Bengal, Andhra Pradesh, Karnataka, Kerala, and Uttar Pradesh (in the district of Allahabad).[91]  Human Rights Watch investigated bonded child labor in the beedi industry of Tamil Nadu only.

Beedi rolling is stationary work;  the children sit cross-legged on the ground or floor all day, with a large and smoothly-woven shallow basket in their laps.  The basket holds a pile of tobacco and a stack of rectangular rolling papers cut from the large leaves of the *tendu* plant.  The child takes a paper, sprinkles tobacco into it, rolls it up tightly, and ties it with string.  The tips are closed either by the roller herself or by a younger child, typically four to seven years old; young children often begin their beedi careers by working as tip closers.

The pace is rapid, with practiced children rolling and tying each beedi cigarette in a matter of seconds.  Most of the older children—those over ten—roll 1,500 to 2,000 beedies each day.  In order to encourage speed, employers keep close vigil over the child workers, scolding them or hitting them if they slow down. Some children have been forced to work with a matchbox tucked between their chin and their neck; in order to hold the box in place, they must keep their head down and focused on the work.  If the matchbox falls, the employer knows the child has looked away and will punish her or him.

Children working under bondage in the beedi industry work between ten and fourteen hours a day, with short breaks for lunch and dinner.  They work six and a half days a week year-round, but are only paid for six—the half day on Sunday is a designated "catching up" day.  When children fail to report to work,

---

[88] "50,000 cr beedies consumed annually," *Indian Express*, February 1, 1995. One crore, abbreviated as "cr," is equal to ten million.

[89] Ibid.

[90] Burra, *Born to Work*, p. xxiv. Another account estimates 248,000 child beedi workers in Tamil Nadu. See R. Vidyasagar,"A Status Report on Child Labour in Tamil Nadu," Madras, 1995, p. 8.

[91] "Children shall be free," *The Hindu*, September 24, 1995; "50,000 cr beedies consumed annually," *Indian Express*, February 1, 1995.

either because of sickness or out of rebellion at the harsh conditions, their employer typically will go to their house and return them to the workplace under force.

### The structure of work and bondage

Entire families are dedicated to the production of beedi. Usually it is the children who work as bonded laborers, with adults managing to buy their own freedom by the time they reach maturity or marry. For these poor families, bondage is a cyclical phase, a defining characteristic of childhood and youth. Generations repeat the steps: as children they are bonded; as young adults they buy or win their release; as mature adults (thirty or thirty-five years is middle-aged in India) they face growing economic pressures—illnesses, weddings and funerals, crop failures, housing needs, alcohol addiction. At the same time that financial need increases, they find their earning power decreasing, as the years of childhood labor take their toll on physical strength and capability. The moneylender-employer offers an advance for the rights to the parent's child, the advance is accepted, and the cycle begins anew.

In other cases, the entire family works in bondage. A regional paper carried the following story:

> When she was six years old, she was pledged for two measures of ragi[92] by her parents to a beedi-rolling agent in their village... Day after day, from dawn to dusk, she rolled beedies for twelve long years. There was no play, no school.

> Today, at thirty, she is still in bondage, rolling beedies. She did have a brief period of respite though. Before marriage, her parents redeemed her. Gouramma was eighteen years old then. But her new found freedom was lost as her alcoholic husband pledged her for Rs 3,000, even before he actually tied the knot. (He had first pledged himself for Rs 4,000.)

> Today the couple has four children, three of them already bonded labourers [aged ten, seven, and five]. If the parents had their way, they would have pledged two year-old Vijayalakshmi, too, but she has no value in the bonded labour market at present.

---

[92] "Ragi" is a type of grain, commonly given to South Indian agricultural laborers instead of cash wages. See R. Vidyasagar, "Debt Bondage in South Arcot District: A Case Study of Agricultural Labourers and Handloom Weavers," *Chains of Servitude*, p. 146.

The parents need not worry: in a year's time the three year-old's nimble fingers will be ready for the work.

The "staggering" sum fetched by the pledging of the entire family is Rs 14,000. "What a life I have led! And what a life I have given my children!" says Gouramma.[93]

The structure of the debt arrangement in the beedi industry is different from that of most other bonded industries, where at least a fraction of the value of the child's labor serves to whittle away at the principal amount owed, at least in theory. (As we will see in discussing the other industries, additional charges and punishments often mean that the debt goes up instead of down.) In beedi, however, the "advances" given to secure the child workers are not paid off by the child's labor, no matter how long she or he works for the bondmaster. In fact, they are not really advances at all, but loans, against which the child's labor functions as both surety and interest.

Whether they are 500 rupees or 4,000 rupees, these loans must be paid back in one lump-sum payment. The child will not be released otherwise, no matter how many thousands of rupees her labor brings to the agent over the years. The lump-sum payback requirement is an extremely harsh condition for the poor, and difficult to meet. Often, the only way a parent can come up with that kind of money is through a loan with another agent or by bonding another child.

Bonded beedi rollers are paid between 20 and 30 percent of the wages they would be entitled to on the open market. The remaining 70 to 80 percent of the value of their wages is kept by the agents, nominally as interest. This system results in effective annual interest rates ranging from 300 to 500 percent. The meager daily wages of the children are further reduced by "penalties," often bogus, for sloppy work or other alleged infractions of workplace rules.

A look at the production and earnings of bonded beedi rollers demonstrates just how lucrative this arrangement is for the bond master.

Twelve-year-old **Raju** was pledged at the age of eight in exchange for a 1,500 rupee loan. He told Human Rights Watch that he rolled 1,000 beedies a day, for which he earned six rupees. The government-established minimum wage for

---

[93] L. R. Jagadheesan, "Whole families are pledged for paltry sums," *Indian Express*, April 25, 1995.

rolling beedi in Tamil Nadu is 30.90 rupees per thousand beedies.[94] After paying Raju his six rupees, then, the agent would have cleared a some twenty-five rupees of profit *every day* if compensated at the minimum wage rate, enough to compensate him for the original loan in a mere two months. Instead, Raju worked for the agent for four years, netting his employer up to 40,000 rupees in the process.

**Kalidasbhai**, thirteen years old, told Human Rights Watch that she earned ten rupees a day for rolling 2,000 beedies, possibly netting his agent more than fifty rupees daily. This is enough money to clear the original debt of 2,000 rupees in a month and a half. Instead, Kalidasbhai is in his seventh year of working for the bond master.

Twelve-year-old **Katankari** earns five rupees a day for rolling 1,500 beedies—her agent keeps the other forty rupees to which she is entitled. Were the value of her labor applied against her parents' original loan of 1,000 rupees, she would be free in three and a half weeks. She told Human Rights Watch that she was in her fifth year of bondage.

These are typical cases. Other children suffer even more severe exploitation. Ten year-old Kumar earned only two rupees a day for rolling 1,500 beedies. The loan taken against him was for 500 rupees. At his rate of production, his original debt obligation should have been canceled in less than two weeks. He worked for his agent for four years before his father, concerned by the agent's abuse of the boy, managed to free him. Several other children interviewed also earned only two or three rupees a day.

Children selling their labor freely earn four, five, or six times as much as their bonded counterparts. Sixteen-year-old Appanraj rolls 1,500 cigarettes a day and earns fifty rupees.[95] Fourteen-year-old Mamta earns forty rupees a day; before

---

[94] The minimum wage for beedi rolling varies from state to state. The wage is slightly lower in Karnataka than in Tamil Nadu, while in the neighboring state of Kerala it is significantly higher, at forty-two rupees per thousand beedi rolled. "50,000 cr beedies consumed annually," *Indian Express*, February 1, 1995. The minimum wage does not apply to children, but is a good indicator of the market value of labor, and non-bonded children in the beedi industry appeared to be receiving wages comparable to the government-set minimum wage. Many activists and some government officials are pressing for legal reform to apply the same minimum wage to adults and children, on the grounds that such a move would decrease child labor and increase adult employment.

[95] This wage is actually 3.65 rupees more than the government set minimum wage for beedi rolling (30.90 rupees per 1,000 beedies). Regardless of whether adults or children roll beedies, they are paid the same on a piece-rate basis. The only wage differentials occur

her liberation by a nongovernmental organization, she earned five to ten rupees a day for the same amount of work. Prabhu, fifteen, was also freed three years ago and saw his earnings quadruple overnight, from nine a day to forty a day. Now that he is compensated for his work, he is able to both pay back the loan that freed him and support his family.

Even these best-off beedi-rolling children lead difficult lives. Prabhu began working in the beedi industry at the age of four in exchange for a 1,500 rupee loan. Initially, he earned one rupee a day. Now he is "free" and works at home; nonetheless, he is marked by exhaustion and defeat.

> I have been working since I was a small child. There is no freedom for me. I want to study—that is my desire, but my parents can not permit it. If I am not working, my family will not live. They are depending on my wages.

### Employer abuse

**Panjaran**, a ten-year-old boy pledged at the age of six for a 500 rupee advance, told Human Rights Watch:

> The agent would beat me with a stick if I was not there on time, he beat me if I could not roll 1,500 beedies a day, and he beat me

---

between bonded and non-bonded beedi rollers. This indicates that there would be no significant difference between adult and child wages when bondage is not a factor or when payment is solely based on production (piece-rate) which is a very common way of paying people in informal occupations where the majority of Indians, children and adults, work. There are other examples of this. For example, in stainless steel factories in Madras, adults and children receive the same piece-rate wages. In Pakistan, where bonded labor is also endemic, adults and children have been paid on the same piece-rate basis in the country's soccer ball industry. These findings call into question a commonly held tenet about child labor: that children's wages depress adult wages in the same industry and that removing children from work would automatically lead to an increase in adult wages. In addition, Neera Burra notes that the piece-rate wage structure in home-based, informal work actually provides an incentive to use children, as their help increases the production, which in-turn provides a higher family income, and says "Unless the issue of home-based, piece-rate workers is resolved and minimum wages and social security provided to this sector, children will continue to be exploited." See Burra, *Born to Work*, p. 255. Removing children from employment would not necessarily result in raising adult wages unless the problems of piece-rate wages and other forms of payment based solely on productivity are addressed as well.

if I was tired. I had to roll eight beedies a minute. If I failed he
would beat me. If I looked around, he beat me. He made me put
a matchbox under my chin; if it fell, he would beat me.

Punishment is common for a variety of infractions: arriving late, working
slowly, making a mistake in the work, talking to other workers—even missing
work because of illness can lead to punishment. With very few exceptions, the
children we interviewed all complained of being beaten and severely scolded. The
beatings consisted of being hit, usually by the agent's open hand, on the arms or
head. A few children reported being beaten by sticks on their arms. The children
clearly resent and fear their agents as a result of this verbal and physical
mistreatment, and the emotional damage of long-term abuse was much in evidence.

Other researchers have found more extreme examples of abuse at the
hands of employers. Until the early 1990s, the matchbox-under-the-chin form of
compulsion and control was quite common, and even measures such as chaining
children in place were not unusual.[96] As recently as 1993, a social worker found
a fourteen-year-old beedi roller who was kept shackled in leg irons. The boy, who
had been bonded for 2,000 rupees, had once attempted to escape, and his employer
had kept him in shackles ever since.[97] Although these forms of abuse have
decreased significantly in villages where social activists have been working to
increase public awareness, there is no evidence to suggest the practices have
changed significantly in more remote villages, where outside intervention has not
taken place.

**Sangeetha**, an eleven-year-old girl, has been in bondage to a beedi agent
for one year, in exchange for an advance of 500 rupees. She works fourteen hours
a day, six and a half days a week, and earns four rupees a day. On November 14,
1995, Sangeetha went to a Children's Day[98] function in a neighboring town, where
participating activists spoke of freeing bonded child laborers. Her agent learned
of Sangeetha's participation and beat her when she returned. Now she is terrified
of him.

---

[96] Human Rights Watch interview with longtime social welfare activist,
November 21, 1995, Madras.

[97] Jacob Varghese, "Freedom at Mid-Day," *Worldvision: A Worldvision of India
Magazine*, Monsoon 1993, p. 6-7.

[98] National Children's Day in India is celebrated on November 14, the birthday
of Jawaharlal Nehru, one of the founding fathers and the first prime minister of India.

### Health hazards

**Kumar**: "Rolling beedi is so hard. We sit all day. My back hurts. I want to be able to play."

Beedi is one of the twenty-five industries classified by the Child Labour (Prohibition and Regulation) Act as hazardous. Beedi rollers suffer chronic back pain from sitting hunched over their work all day. The long hours of maintaining this unnatural position sometimes interfere with normal growth patterns, causing stunted growth or physical deformities among those who spend their childhoods rolling beedi. As adults, these children will be restricted in the types of work they are physically able to do; they will not be able to perform hard manual labor and may in fact be restricted to beedi rolling for their entire productive lives.[99] Large muscle groups are neglected and atrophy during years of sitting six and a half days a week, for twelve or more hours a day. In the words of one local beedi activist, the children grow up "small, puny, and malnourished."[100]

In addition to back ailments, many of the children interviewed by Human Rights Watch complained of pain in their hands and wrists, which suffer from the constant repetitive motion of rolling and tying the cigarettes. "My hands would hurt so bad sometimes I thought I couldn't work," said Chintamani, a twelve-year-old boy who had been rolling beedies for three years. But, as Chintamani's mother pointed out, he had to work despite the pain. "If the child misses work because he is in pain or sick with fever or disease, the agent will beat him and take him back," she told Human Rights Watch.

The damage to the body is cumulative and progressive. "As the worker gets older her/his fingers become numb and, unlike a young worker, an older worker has to make three or four attempts to roll a beedi. The nature of beedi work is such that a worker cannot take his/her eyes off it even for a moment if he/she is to make the required number of beedies for a day. This takes its toll on people's eyesight as they grow older."[101]

The most serious health hazard of the beedi industry is lung disease. Beedi rollers spend their lives constantly inhaling tobacco dust, and study after study has shown them to suffer a high rate of tuberculosis, asthma, and other lung

---

[99] Human Rights Watch interview with social welfare activist, November 21, 1995, Madras.

[100] Ibid.

[101] Vidyasagar,"A Status Report...," p. 9.

disorders.[102] Of the twenty-six child beedi rollers interviewed by Human Rights Watch, six (23 percent) had parents who were either dead or dying as a result of tuberculosis.[103] If the cycle continues unchanged, in twenty-five years these children will themselves be dying, while their own sons and daughters breathe tobacco dust and grow feeble.

### *Applicable domestic law*

The trend over the last three decades has been one of increasing decentralization of beedi production. The main reason for this has been the evasion of legal obligations, since nearly all legislative safeguards and restrictions apply only to formal work sites—factories, "industrial premises," and the like. Beedi rolling that occurs in a home environment—whether it be the home of the worker or not—is not covered by the two primary labor welfare laws affecting beedi rollers: the Child Labour (Prohibition and Regulation) Act of 1986, and the Beedi and Cigar Workers (Conditions of Employment) Act of 1966.

### The Beedi and Cigar Workers (Conditions of Employment) Act of 1966

The Beedi and Cigar Workers Act (Beedi Act) was enacted by the central government in response to a beedi workers' movement mounted in the early 1960s in Tamil Nadu. The Beedi Act prohibits the employment of children under fourteen in any beedi or cigar factory. It also sets maximum hours of work (nine hours a day and forty-eight hours a week), prescribes half-hour rest intervals after five hours of work, and limits the work week to six days. In the case of child workers, the Beedi Act puts the onus of proof of age on the employer—an example the writers of the Child Labour (Prohibition and Regulation) Act inexplicably and unfortunately chose not to follow.

For the child laborer, however, and for most adult beedi rollers as well, these protections are for naught. The Beedi Act safeguards the rights only of those working in "industrial premises," defined as "any place or premises (*not being a*

---

[102] Ibid. Vidyasagar cites a study of one beedi manufacturing village that found 25 percent of all beedi rollers to have tuberculosis.

[103] Human Rights Watch interviews, North Arcot district, Tamil Nadu, November 25, 1995.

*private dwelling-house*)," (emphasis added) where the beedi process is carried on, with or without the use of power.[104]

Not surprisingly, after passage of this protective measure, the beedi manufacturing units began to disperse. Large rolling centers were disbanded and the contract system grew.[105] Under this system, the owner distributes tobacco and tendu leaves to middlemen, who in turn contract local agents. These agents either employ beedi rollers directly, in the agent's home, or farm the work out to daily wage laborers. Those who work out of their own homes usually do so with the help of family members (the youngest child may close the tips, another may cut the leaves, and so on). These extremely decentralized processes free the owner and his agents from worrying about compliance with the law.

### The Child Labour (Prohibition and Regulation) Act

As with the Beedi Act, glaring loopholes in the Child Labour (Prohibition and Regulation) Act allow manufacturers to escape application of the law quite easily. After passage of the Child Labour (Prohibition and Regulation) Act, the beedi industry intentionally fragmented itself even further in order to avoid coming within the terms of the act. By 1996, approximately 90 percent of beedi rolling took place in private homes, either the house of a contracted worker or the house of the contracting agent. In the former case, a child working with one or both parents would not be protected by the Child Labour (Prohibition and Regulation) Act. In the latter case, a child worker would theoretically be protected by the act. However, contracting agents frequently lie, claiming that the children are relatives in order to avoid application of the law.

### The Bonded Labour System (Abolition) Act
### The Children (Pledging of Labour) Act

Both acts are violated by the practice of debt servitude in the beedi industry.

---

[104] Beedi and Cigar Workers (Conditions of Employment) Act, 1966, Sec. 2(I).

[105] Asha Krishnakumar, "Reprehensible by any name: Children in beedi industry," *Frontline* (Madras), November 17, 1995, p. 87.

### Enforcement: the North Arcot District Collector's scheme

The North Arcot district of Tamil Nadu is home to some of the worst and most extensive bondage of child beedi rollers in the country.[106] Of the 150,000 beedi workers in that district, an estimated 30,000 to 45,000 are bonded child laborers.[107] Entire clusters of villages are given over to the production of beedi, and to walk through these villages is to see evidence of the industry everywhere. Children sit rolling cigarettes under trees and in doorways, to catch the light. Large baskets stuffed full of bundles of beedies sit near agents' doors. Stacks of uncut *tendu* leaves and piles of tobacco in the morning become a box full of thousands of cigarettes by the night. It appears that every second person on the street, from the very young to the very old, has the tips of his or her fingers stained a deep orange brown. Beedi is a way of life in these towns of North Arcot, and so is bondage.

In the spring of 1995, the district collector for North Arcot initiated a scheme for combating this high rate of child bondage. Denominated CLASS, for Child Labour Abolition Support Scheme, the program pulls together resources from already-existing government programs, such as the Integrated Rural Development Programme, the Drought Prone Areas Programme, and the Development of Women and Children in Rural Areas program, and directs them toward a focused attack on bonded child labor in the beedi industry. It is the first and only program of its kind currently in operation in India.

District Collector M. P. Vijaykumar began the CLASS campaign by organizing a child labor census. Ten thousand village literacy volunteers were mobilized, and on April 14, 1995, they conducted a one-day survey of 313,940 households in North Arcot. The overall results of the census have not yet been released, but the collector did make public the data for one representative beedi village, Kasikuttai, which was chosen to be a model for the scheme's

---

[106] Vidyasagar, "Status Report...," p. 8.

[107] Local government authorities estimate there are 45,000 bonded child laborers in the North Arcot district alone, most working in the beedi industry. "Child Labour Abolition Support Scheme (A proposal submitted to the International Labour Organisation)," North Arcot Ambedkar District, 1995, p. 1. An estimated 30,000 bonded children work in the beedi industry in North Arcot. See Vidyasagar, "A Status Report...," p. 8. Unlike most beedi-producing areas, where 90 percent of the workers are women and children, North Arcot district has a significant percentage of adult male beedi workers. Vidyasagar attributes the high rate of bondage in North Arcot to the presence of men workers in the same industry, hypothesizing that "men use children's labour to augment their income by keeping them under bondage by paying low wages." Ibid.

implementation. The survey found that 159 of Kasikuttai's 174 families were engaged in the beedi industry; sixty-six of these families had children under the age of fourteen working in the production of beedi; and, of these 102 child beedi workers, forty-one were in bondage.[108]

The collector estimated that in 1995, 1,000 of the 5,000 hamlets in North Arcot district had a significant bonded child labor problem.[109] His immediate goal was to establish CLASS programs in one hundred of these villages, working on behalf of an estimated 7,000 bonded child laborers.[110] When Human Rights Watch met with District Collector Vijaykumar in late November 1995, he claimed to be operating CLASS initiatives in forty-three villages. In these project areas of North Arcot, 1,455 children reportedly had been released from bondage by the end of October 1995.[111]

Whether those children ostensibly released from bondage under the collector's scheme actually go free, or are able to remain free, is another matter. Human Rights Watch visited several of the beedi villages where CLASS was operative and spoke with children "liberated" under the program, as well as with local activists, schoolteachers, and government administrators. We discovered that approximately 30 percent of all the children "freed" by the collector were in fact still working in servitude to their bond masters. Some of these children worked full-time for the agents, as before, while others worked before and after school, beginning their days at 6:00 a.m. at the agent's house and ending there at 9:00 p.m. With only one exception, the length of additional servitude was indeterminate and at the agent's discretion.

When the CLASS program began in the first few villages, the collector approached agents employing bonded child labor and offered to compensate them at 50 percent of the original loan amount in exchange for the release of the bonded children. (The money was to be paid not by the government, but out of a local women's savings and loan scheme facilitated and supported by the government, with some government financial contributions.) The amount of 50 percent was

---

[108] "Child labour census in Tamil Nadu district," *The Hindu*, April 28, 1995.

[109] "Child Labour Abolition Support Scheme (A proposal submitted to the International Labour Organisation)," North Arcot Ambedkar District, 1995, p. 8.

[110] Ibid. pp. 1, 8-12, and 25.

[111] Human Rights Watch interview with North Arcot District Collector M. P. Vijaykumar, November 27, 1995, Vellore, Tamil Nadu.

proposed not as a compromise between full repayment (honoring the status quo) versus zero repayment and prosecution of the offending agents (strict application of the law), but as an amount that purported to reflect what the agents would be entitled to had they offset the original loans against a reasonable value of the children's labor. Collector Vijaykumar threatened to prosecute those bond masters who did not accept this offer.[112]

In the villages visited by Human Rights Watch, the agents had accepted the offer, but not all of them had honored it.

The continuing compulsion of children whom the collector had purportedly freed was common knowledge, including among the CLASS administrators and teachers. When we told District Collector Vijaykumar about the ongoing bondage in his model villages, he admitted knowing that children were still working mornings and nights to pay the other half of the original loans, but seemed undisturbed by this state of affairs. He revealed no intention of prosecuting these recalcitrant agents, or even of going to the nearby village to talk to them. In fact, despite this knowledge of ongoing servitude, both he and CLASS staff continued to refer to these villages as "bonded labor-free. "The high failure rate of the collector's scheme can be attributed to the traditional acceptance of debt bondage by all sectors of society. It can be attributed as well to the collector's own participation in the system, a participation revealed by his reluctance to prosecute, his refusal to free the children outright despite having the legal mandate to do so, and his conciliatory approach to the bond masters, including treating the bond debts as valid and legitimate.

The following description of the CLASS program reveals its conservative and timid nature. That this is the boldest program in the country is a discouraging testament to the government's low prioritization of recovering children from bonded labor.

---

[112] Depending on the circumstances of the case, a bondmaster could be charged under the Bonded Labour System (Abolition) Act, the Child Labour (Prohibition and Regulation) Act, or the Factories Act. As of 1995, the collector had initiated a limited number of prosecutions under all three laws, including a handful of cases against parents who had bonded their children. Human Rights Watch interview with North Arcot District Collector M. P. Vijaykumar, November 27, 1995, Vellore, Tamil Nadu; "Project Proposal for Community-Based Convergent Services," North Arcot Ambedkar District, June, 1995, p. 15 Most activists agree that prosecution of parents is misguided. Among prosecuted employers, as of December 1995 the collector had not aimed for prison sentences, but instead sought only modest fines.

The CLASS program has four prongs, of which rehabilitation of the child worker is only one. The other three are: improving the incomes and savings of at-risk families, fostering social and attitudinal changes in these families, and placing the liberated children into educational or vocational training programs. The overall thrust of the program is not to bring an immediate halt to the illegal bondage and exploitation of child workers by their agents, for example through enforcement of the Bonded Labour System (Abolition) Act. Instead, the emphasis is on a long-term transformation of the poorest beedi-rolling families: encouraging them to save, providing support to their attempts to free their daughters and sons, and making greater educational opportunities available to their children. The scheme is attempting to break the cycle of poverty that results in endemic bondage.

In all this, the initiative is important and laudable. At the same time, it is alarmingly acquiescent to the agents and owners of the beedi industry and to the status quo.

The CLASS project proposes to rehabilitate children from bondage by:

Staggered repayment of the borrowings from middlemen with the aid of loans from the Group Support Fund made up of the mothers' savings and the matching grant from the project.

Institutional support in dealings with the middlemen and in eliciting their cooperation.

Attitudinal changes within the families about the need and the ability to dispense with  bonded child labour in favour of primary education and vocational training.[113]

The Bonded Labour System (Abolition) Act is unequivocal. It declares illegal any agreement purporting to exchange labor for a loan, and where such debts do exist, it extinguishes them. It subjects employers or others who attempt to make or enforce debt bondage agreements to a fine of up to 2,000 rupees, or three years in prison, or both. Furthermore, and most significant for this discussion, "[b]y making the offences cognizable under the act, the State has undertaken the *direct responsibility* for the implementation of the act, and . . . does

---

[113] North Arcot Ambedkar District, "Child Labour Abolition Support Scheme (CLASS)," Proposal submitted to International Labour Organisation, 1995, p. 10.

not leave it to the initiative of the affected individuals."[114] In fact, the act can *only* by applied by government officials in the form of criminal proceedings—the act specifically precludes civil court jurisdiction. In other words, the state has adopted full responsibility for eradicating bonded labor. This obligation is not being met in the vast majority of districts, where absolutely no attempts have been made to thwart the bondmasters. Nor is it being met in North Arcot district, the model district of the state of Tamil Nadu and of the country overall.

At the same time, the CLASS program has created a positive precedent for at least some government action. District Collector Vijaykumar and the numerous civil servants working with him to create and sustain the CLASS program together constitute an irrefutable example that it is possible for government to combat bonded child labor. What is more, the collector has insisted that other government administrators cannot excuse their inaction as a function of lack of resources. "Resources are not the issue," he told Human Rights Watch. "The existing schemes provide enough money and personnel. The issue is commitment."[115]

**Mani**, a thirteen-year-old boy, has been in bondage since the age of six, when his parents accepted a 2,000 rupee loan in order to build a house. He spent seven years working ten hours a day, six and a half days a week.

Mani was one of the children in his village to be released in late 1995 under the North Arcot District Collector's scheme. After his ostensible release, the agent he worked for came to his house and told him that he still owed 1,000 rupees and that he must work mornings and nights to pay it off. Consequently, Mani now works for three hours before school and for three hours after, rolling 1,000 beedies a day, for which he is paid five rupees. He also works Sundays half days, without pay. He told Human Rights Watch:

> I have to work until the debt is settled; I don't know when that will be. My father is disabled. The agent takes advantage of me because he sees that there is no support. My income is the only income we have, that is why I have to work. My family scolds me for going to school.

**Munirathna**, a twelve-year-old girl, was sold into bondage when her father died in 1993. Like Mani, she was one of the children freed by the collector

---

[114] Reddy, *Bonded Labour System in India*, p. 56.

[115] Human Rights Watch interview with North Arcot District Collector M. P. Vijaykumar, November 27, 1995, Vellore, Tamil Nadu.

in late 1995; he arranged for payment of half of the 1,000 rupee advance given for Munirathna. Also like Mani, Munirathna's agent refused to release her, claiming that she still owed him the other 500 rupees. She continues to work for the bond master ten hours a day, six and a half days a week. She is paid twenty rupees a week.

There are six children in Munirathna's family: two boys and four girls. One boy studies and one is an electrical worker. Munirathna is the oldest of the girls, all of whom roll beedi. Five of Munirathna's friends also continue working in servitude despite the intervention of the collector.

> I am very sad that my father died; so is my mother. Whenever
> I go to work for the agent he scolds me. I am very sad with my
> life.

**Ramesh**, a thirteen-year-old boy, was put into bondage in 1993 for a 2,500 rupee advance; his parents took the money so they could build a house. Ramesh was working six and a half days a week, from 7:00 a.m. until 9:00 p.m., rolling 1,500 beedies a day. If he rolled less than 1,500 cigarettes, the agent would beat him.

Although "freed" by the collector, Ramesh continues to work for the agent before and after school. Instead of working fourteen hours a day he now works from 6:00 to 9:00 a.m. and from 5:00 to 6:00 p.m., rolling 500 beedies a day and earning five rupees. Ramesh told Human Rights Watch:

> I don't like to roll beedies—my hands get stiff and hurt, and I
> would rather be studying. But the collector only settled half of
> the debt, so I have to work to pay the rest.

In 1991, the Supreme Court of India ordered that child labor in tobacco manufacturing units, which threaten childrens' health, should be prohibited. In addition, the court ordered state governments to formulate a plan to either end child labor immediately or phase children out of the beedi industry, within three years. By mid-1996, no such plans had been implemented.[116]

---

[116] Vidyasagar, "A Status Report ...," p.9.

## SILVER

The city of Salem, Tamil Nadu has been a major producer of domestically-consumed silver jewelry[117] since 1980. Of the 100,000 child laborers working in Salem district,[118] an estimated 10,000 are working in silver smithies.[119] These workers are concentrated in towns given over largely to the silver industry, augmenting the dwindling possibilities of subsistence agriculture. In the town Human Rights Watch visited, there were five hundred residents, two hundred of whom were children under the age of fifteen. One hundred and thirty-five of these children were laboring in the production of silver.[120] It is reported to be an entirely bonded industry.[121]

Boys and girls enter the industry in equal numbers, usually between the ages of six and eight but occasionally as young as five years old. Most remain bonded and continue working in the silver industry throughout childhood and adolescence. During this time, they may move from employer to employer, receiving a bigger advance from their new employer so that they might both pay off their previous employer and enjoy a small—and temporary—boost in their cash flow. This new and higher debt must then be worked off, or passed on to a younger sibling when the worker leaves the employer. All girl workers expect to leave their jobs at the time of marriage. Young men may try to eke out a living through

---

[117] The "silver" referred to throughout this discussion is not pure silver, but a blend of silver and lesser metals.

[118] The figure of 100,000 working children in Salem is based on a social scientist's finding that Salem district accounts for 10.93 percent of all child workers in the state of Tamil Nadu, and the 1981 census figures of 975,055 working children, below the age of fourteen, in Tamil Nadu. See Vidyasagar, "A Status Report....," pp. 2-3. Based on more reliable statistics and analyses, however, Vidyasagar himself estimates that there are four million working children in Tamil Nadu, which would indicate about 400,000 child laborers in Salem district alone. Ibid., p. 5.

[119] Ibid., p. 14.

[120] Human Rights Watch interview with the chief of a village near Salem, Tamil Nadu, November 30, 1995.

[121] Background information on the silver industry of Salem was provided during a Human Rights Watch interview with staff members of a local nongovernmental organization, November 30, 1995. It requested anonymity in order to avoid possible repercussions against its programs or staff.

agriculture, or stay in silver and work their way up the wage scale. The maximum pay for a non-bonded man with twenty-five years of experience is forty rupees a day.

In addition to maintaining a cheap and compliant workforce, another impetus for bondage is the silversmiths' desire to maintain a skilled, productive worker. In many cases, an advance is not immediately offered to the parents of the child. Instead, parents contact agents or agents offer to "train" children on the pretense of teaching children a marketable skill. Parents, believing this will be beneficial for their children, agree. The child is then made to work as an apprentice for approximately six months to a year. The length of the training period is largely based on the child's ability to learn. During this time, the child is paid about two rupees per day. The advance is not offered to the parents until after the initial training period. This training period allows owners to spot children that may be especially productive or who have a natural aptitude for the work. In this respect, the bonded labor system in the silver industry has evolved to the point of incorporating a screening process for children.[122]

The average advance for a six-year-old is 5,000 rupees. Although interest is not added to the principal amount owed, the disparity between the extremely low rate of wages paid and the minimum wage is equivalent to an effective annual interest rates in the range of 300 percent. Beginning children earn one to five rupees a day, while accomplished child workers earn ten rupees a day. Bonded workers fifteen and older can make as much as twenty or twenty-five rupees a day; these wages reflect ten years or more of experience.

Unlike beedi, agents in the silver industry do allow gradual repayment of the initial advance. Given the low wages paid, however, only the oldest and most skilled workers stand a chance of actually paying back their loans. In some cases, the ability for a child to pay back the loan is largely based on the silversmith's opinion of the child, as one employer told us:

> If the child is good and works hard and is reliable we let them pay back the loan on time, but if they are lazy or don't do enough work, it will take them a lot longer to repay it.[123]

---

[122] Human Rights Watch interview with a social worker who works with the children in this industry, Salem, November 28, 1995.

[123] Human Rights Watch interview with a small-scale silver smithy owner who, at the time of the interview, had three bonded children working, Salem, November 30, 1995.

Depending on the employer, children work six days a week, six and a half days a week, or twenty-eight days a month, with the days of the new and full moon off. The typical work day is twelve hours long, from 8:00 a.m. to 8:00 p.m. This increases by up to four hours a day during the two or three months preceding Diwali, the "festival of the lights." Diwali usually falls in late October or early November.

### Health hazards and employer abuses

Children work in a variety of jewelry-making phases. They create linked chains by cutting circles of silver from a tightly coiled rod and hooking them into each other. They flatten chains with heavy hammers, preparing them to be decorated with silver flowers and other adornments. They solder the decorations on to the jewelry, and they weld on hooks and screws and other fasteners. Children also polish and finish the pieces of jewelry, turning them from dark brown metal into gleaming trinkets. Each one of these processes carries its own risk. Several children interviewed showed us their work scars: cuts and burns on their fingers, hands, arms, legs, and feet. These injuries are caused by the metal and metalworking tools used to cut and fashion jewelry, the blowtorches used to weld it, and the acid mixes used to polish the final silver product.

The detail work of cutting and fashioning chains creates eye strain and headache. This is exacerbated by the requirement that the children remain still for long periods of time and work quickly, with intense concentration. One boy showed us how to make a chain. In less than two minutes he had created four inches of chain, rapidly snapping the tiny circles off the rod and just as quickly pinching them together with a pair of pincer pliers. Children are expected to maintain this pace during their twelve hours or more of work. In addition to the damage this causes to the eyes, there is a constant danger of cuts to the children's hands and fingers, which are continually exposed to sharp tools and to the points and edges of unfinished metal.

Welding poses a more serious threat to the eyes. The children are given no protective masks or goggles of any kind, and the blowtorches used are primitive contraptions, fueled by kerosene and with an unregulated flame. Because it is detail work, as the children weld they must keep their eyes near the point of junction, looking straight into the flame. Welders' eyes sting and tear and their vision becomes blurry. Several children told us that this was their primary health concern. Burns from welding and falling pieces of hot metal are other routine workplace dangers.

The jewelry-polishing process is extremely hazardous. It requires children to drop the completed pieces into sulfuric acid ($H_2SO_4$) until they turn the bright white of silver. Wearing no protective gloves, they have to mix the acid as well, and during both the mixing and the polishing stages suffer chemical burns on their hands, arms, legs, and feet. Other children told of hammer heads flying off without warning and of sparks flying into their eyes during welding.

Long-term health hazards include lung diseases, caused by breathing the sulphuric acid fumes; tuberculosis, caused by the cramped and unsanitary conditions; and physical deformities, particularly of the back, caused by the long years of working in a hunched and still position.

### Applicable domestic law

#### The Factories Act

Although silver is a cottage industry in Salem, the size of the manufacturing units is sometimes large enough to bring them under the purview of the Factories Act.[124] Several of the children interviewed reported working in factories of more than ten employees, and one reported working in a factory employing twenty-five children and a number of adults. Because even small shops rely on the use of power for soldering, the Factories Act would apply in both such cases.

The act not only prohibits the employment of children, but also sets forth health and safety guidelines that are routinely violated by the conditions and practices of the silver smithies. These include ventilation requirements where injurious fumes are present (Sec. 14); a prohibition on the use of dangerous machines by children and adolescents (Sec. 23); and limitations on exposure to chemical and toxic substances (Sec. 41-F). Stipulated working hours and periods of rest (Secs. 51 - 55, Sec. 71) are also flouted as a matter of course.

#### The Child Labour (Prohibition and Regulation) Act

Silver working is not a prohibited occupation for children under the Child Labour (Prohibition and Regulation) Act. The Child Labour (Prohibition and Regulation) Act's regulations regarding the conditions of work by children do apply, however, and are violated across the board by the employer practices described above. Provisions violated include the right to an hour of rest after three hours of work; a maximum work day of six hours; a prohibition on child work before 8:00 a.m. or after 7:00 p.m.; a prohibition on overtime; a mandatory day of rest every week; and the requirement that various health and safety precautions be observed.

---

[124] See chapter on applicable law.

**The Bonded Labour System (Abolition) Act**
**The Children (Pledging of Labour) Act**
Both acts are violated by the practice of debt servitude in the silver industry.

*Enforcement*

As of December 1995, there had been no effort by any government official to inspect or control these factories or to enforce the legal prohibitions on bonded labor. According to local activists, the Salem district collector was planning to start a "special school" for child laborers in 1996, with financial assistance from UNICEF.

Speaking on behalf of District Collector Hans Rej Verma, the Salem district project officer for child labor confirmed that the district had begun a program of five non-formal education centers, each to attend to fifty child workers.[125] The schools were to provide these 250 children with three hours of non-formal schooling in the evenings after work, teaching them "practical and useful" skills. The beneficiaries would be drawn from the four main industries employing child labor in the area: beedi, textiles, silver jewelry, and tapioca.

This initiative—for part-time "practical" education for a relative handful of child workers—appeared to be the district's only initiative *vis à vis* its child labor problem. According to the collector's office, as of December 1995 there had been no prosecutions under either the Bonded Labour System (Abolition) Act or the Child Labour (Prohibition and Regulation) Act, and no prosecutions for child labor violations under the Factories Act.[126]

The district's project officer on child labor told Human Rights Watch: "In Salem totally there are no bonded labourer children. Definitely not."[127]

---

[125] Human Rights Watch telephone interview with Project Officer J. L. Poland, December 1, 1995, Salem, Tamil Nadu. The district government's goal was to establish twenty such schools, with one hundred working children in each.

[126] Ibid. Instead of prosecuting, the office is employing a "cooperative approach" and "working with the companies [that employ child laborers]," according to the project officer. A local activist put this another way. "He [the district collector] is collaborating with the big mill and factory owners.... They [government officials] will never worry about the welfare of the child labourers." Human Rights Watch interview, November 30, 1995.

[127] Ibid.

***Testimonies Given to Human Rights Watch by Bonded Child Silver Workers in Salem***

**Selvakumar**, a twelve-year-old boy, was sent by his parents to the silversmith at the age of eight because he was "not studying properly." They received a 3,000 rupee advance for their son; his mother later approached the employer for additional loans, which he gave her. Selvakumar's work schedule varied according to the season. During the months leading up to the holiday of Diwali, the workers are driven at a furious pace, and Selvakumar worked from 7:30 a.m. until midnight or 1:00 a.m. the following morning. After the holidays, the demand for silver drops, and the silver shops return to an 8:00 a.m. to 8:00 p.m. schedule. At the time he left the shop, Selvakumar was earning 350 rupees a month.

He described the work as very difficult and very hot. His job was to solder small decorative flowers to the jewelry and solder screws on to earrings. "Very small pieces have to be placed in very small and precise spots. We used a small wire for this job, like a bicycle spoke. Sometimes the owner would beat me with this hot wire if he thought I wasn't working properly. He would take the wire and beat me on the arms."

After three years, Selvakumar ran away from the factory. The first time he ran away, an older brother found him and brought him back. The second time, the owner found him at a shelter for street children, but the shelter's director refused to turn him over to the man. His mother then came and took him back to the factory, but he did not last long. He ran away a third and final time. Selvakumar did not return to his parents' house and assumed that they had to pay back the original loan. Selvakumar was interviewed by Human Rights Watch at a shelter for street children.

**Manojan**, also twelve, could not remember when he began working, only that it was a long time ago. When Human Rights Watch interviewed him, he worked as a solderer, sitting in one spot all day long, from 8:00 a.m. until 8:00 at night. He worked with a crude blowtorch, welding together the tiny silver links and decorations of bracelets and necklaces. He had no mask to protect him from the flame, and his eyes teared continuously from staring at the junction of flame and fine metal pieces. He earned ten rupees a day.

Manojan's four brothers also worked in the silver smithies. His sister, the eldest child, also worked in silver, until she married. Then she left the industry and a young brother was brought in to assume her duty of debt. Manojan became bonded for a 2,000 rupee advance, his sister for one of 3,000 rupees. She was bonded eight years ago. Despite her eight years of work for wages one-third of the average minimum wage, her debt to the bondmaster was never reduced; when her younger brother took her place, he inherited her full original debt.


Manojan sang a song, which he learned at the non-formal education center:

> *My mother is crying;*
> *I'm working in a silver smithy at the age of six.*
> *When I went to school the teacher opposed me—"You can't study here! Go home!"*
> *Now I am as if blind.*
> *You send me to the factory because we are poor. But we will always be poor.*
> *You send me to the factory to earn a regular income. But instead of regular income, I carry the heavy burden of a loan.*
> *This loan burden is my poison.*

**Vennila**, a fifteen-year-old girl, had been working in the silver industry for five years when Human Rights Watch interviewed her. Twenty-five people worked in her factory (enough to bring it under the provisions of the Factories Act). The workers ranged in age from five to fifteen and earned between five and twenty-five rupees a day. She herself earned twenty rupees a day.

She and her brother were bonded at the same time in exchange for a 10,000 rupee advance. Her parents needed the money to pay off a loan from the local moneylender, who charged an interest rate of 20 percent. She worked from 8:00 a.m. to 7:00 p.m., six days a week. She planned to stop working when she married, leaving her brother to repay the total debt.

> We lost all our chances at an early age. When I'm working in the shop, I can see the children going by to school. I wish I were with those school-going children.

**Dhanraj**, a nine-year-old, showed us the burn scars on his arms. He began working at the age of six. Dhanraj was bonded together with his three siblings after his father fell ill from emphysema. The four children together netted an advance of 14,000 rupees.

**Ramchandran**, working in silver since the age of five, was fifteen years old when interviewed by Human Rights Watch. He earned twenty rupees a day, working eleven hours a day, six days a week. He was taken to his first master by his father, who received 100 rupees in exchange. In late 1995 he owed 4,000 rupees, which he was paying back at the rate of 300 rupees a month—half of his salary. He hated the work but knew he could not leave until the debt was cleared.

**Papu** claimed to be seven but had the body of a four-year-old. He worked eleven hours a day, for which he earned two rupees. He knew that his father received some money when Papu was first taken to the master, but he did not know how much it was.

**Shabnam**, a thirteen-year-old girl, had been working in the silver factories for eight years. She worked all day, with a half-hour for lunch, and earned thirteen rupees. She was pledged together with her brother for an 8,000 rupee advance. If the master had applied but one and a half rupees per day of work toward liquidation of their debt—an amount that would have still left him with the lion's share of unpaid market-rate wages—both she and her brother would have been freed after eight years. Instead, she told Human Rights Watch that they could see no end in sight to their bondage.

## SYNTHETIC GEMSTONES

Gem cutting and polishing is a traditional cottage-based industry. The introduction of synthetic gems is fairly recent, however, with the Tiruchirappalli (Trichy) synthetic gem industry dating back only to the late 1980s. Approximately 95 percent of the total workers in this industry are bonded and non-bonded women. Even though this is a relatively young industry, the bonded labor system has managed to adapt and evolve with it as an estimated 100,000 of the 160,000 workers in this industry are believed to be bonded.[128] Bonded child laborers in the synthetic gem industry number between 8,000 and 10,000.[129] Nearly all of them are members of the scheduled castes.[130]

Synthetic gemstones are cut and polished in two districts of Tamil Nadu—Trichy and Pudukottai. The industry produces for both domestic and export

---

[128] *Report of the Commission on Bonded Labour in Tamilnadu*, submitted to the Supreme Court for Supreme Court Civ. Writ Petition No. 3922 of 1985. October 31, 1995, Madras, Tamil Nadu, p. 75.

[129] Vidyasagar, "A Status Report...," p. 12.

[130] *Report of the Commission on Bonded Labour in Tamilnadu*, p. 76. Those few gem workers who are not scheduled caste members are members of lower castes.

markets; its main product, the "American diamond" (cubic zirconium), generates annual revenues of 100 million rupees, or about three million U.S. dollars.[131]

The government of India has actively promoted the growth of the synthetic gem industry. In 1990, it launched a scheme announced to be intended to combat unemployment in the Trichy area while boosting production of American diamonds. The scheme included the establishment of a "gem park" in the city, an institution devoted to "introducing the latest technology in cutting and polishing of American diamonds."[132] This new technology was brought in to replace the traditional methods, which were deemed to be unacceptable to the international market.[133] The government offered local artisans "scientific training" in the new methods, marketing support, and financial "assistance" in buying "the latest semi-automatic machines . . to make uniform calibrated stones."[134] Most of the participants in this scheme have been rural women.

A serious government oversight in undertaking this scheme was the failure to foresee its practical effect of increasing child labor.[135] There is a tendency for

---

[131] "A training centre on synthetic diamonds production," *The Free Press Journal*, January 16, 1996.

[132] Ibid.

[133] Ibid.

[134] Ibid.

[135] There have been several other problems with this initiative. According to the director of a local social welfare organization, the new machines, which the government encouraged people to buy, were very expensive (valued at 8,000 rupees each) and were sold to participants by government agents at an inflated price (up to 16,000 rupees each). These purchases were financed by bank loans set up with government assistance, and buyers were then saddled with long-term bank debts. A second problem was over saturation of the market as a direct result of the gem park scheme. More than 6,000 people bought these machines and were trained to use them. Many of these buyers were entering into the industry for the first time, enticed by government promises of steady earnings. With more and more American diamonds being produced, a glut in the market soon developed. Within a year, many of the machines stood idle, their owners having defaulted on the loans and begun looking for other means of income generation. Another accusation against the program is that the training process has been inadequate, with the result that some participants never even learned how to use their machines. Some machines, then, were idle from the start. That the production glut happened anyway underscores an even greater potential for market flooding.

women workers' children to work alongside them, assisting in the process and thereby boosting the piece-rate wages, and frequently gem workers' young children accompany them and assist them with their work. In this case, the government encouraged more women to enter the gem industry without taking steps to limit the influx of child workers. Safeguards against increasing child labor could have included the facilitation of school attendance, the providing of incentives for women to refrain from using their children in the workplace, or ensuring that the development of this industry was in compliance with Article 43 of the Indian Constitution, which states:

> The State shall endeavour to secure, by suitable legislation or economic organization or in any other way, to all workers, agricultural, industrial or otherwise, work, a living wage, conditions of work ensuring a decent standard of life and full enjoyment of leisure and social and cultural opportunities and, in particular, the State shall endeavour to promote cottage industries on an individual or cooperative basis in rural areas.

There are a minimum of four layers in the production of synthetic gemstones: the jewelry merchant; the producer, who ensures available product for the market; the middleman, who secures the workers, often through debt bondage or an essential analog; and the worker. Production is decentralized, taking place primarily in small workshops and private homes.

The gem industry is labor intensive, with every stage of the process requiring careful attention. Some workers labor on their own machines (see "government scheme," below), while others work in factories of up to twenty machines. Older children are likely to be themselves bonded and working independently for a master. This practice of family "help" is encouraged by the piece-rate wage system.

### Structure of Bondage

Most bonded workers earn about 50 percent of the free-market wage rate.[136] In real terms, they earn fifty to sixty paise (one hundred paise to a rupee) per stone, which will sell on the market for eight or nine rupees each. According to nongovernmental organizations active in the area, most bonded workers do not know the market value of the stones they are producing or of their labor. Often they do not even know the cost of the raw materials, a cost which is inflated and

---

[136] *Report of the Commission on Bonded Labour in Tamilnadu*, p. 76.

either deducted from their pay or added to their loan obligation. The middlemen/lenders keep them ignorant by interceding on both sides of the production process: the middleman supplies the materials, and the middleman buys the finished stones. It is common for the middleman/lender to pay for only 75 percent of the stones produced, claiming that the remainder are defective. Also, he pays at a rate set by himself and non-negotiable by the workers. Through this system, even those laborers who are not overtly bonded are in a perpetual state of indirect bondage. They are advanced the cost of materials, but, by inflating this cost and deflating wages, the lender manages to keep them in constant and ever-increasing debt.

Bondage for children begins at the age of seven or eight. An employer will give between five and eight thousand rupees for a child. As in other industries, parents tend to take these loans to meet daily needs and to cover the cost of special or unforeseen events—weddings and funerals, house construction, illnesses, and so on. In the gem industry, they also take these advances in order to buy raw materials for their own production efforts. The advances can be paid off gradually, but a high rate of interest is charged.

Human Rights Watch interviewed two bonded child laborers in the gem industry, a nine-year-old girl and a twelve-year-old girl. The twelve-year-old girl earned less than two rupees a day, while the nine-year-old did not know how much she earned, since her wages, if any, went directly to her parents. Both girls were bonded, but neither knew the amount of the original advance.

Lenders not only exploit the financial need of the gem workers, but enhance it through manipulation of the gem market. During September, October, and November, before the Diwali holiday, the gem agents refuse to buy the finished stones, saying there is no market for them. This is a concerted effort by all of the agents to create a glut in the market, enabling them to sweep back in at Diwali-time and buy up stones at an artificially-depressed price. This cycle repeats every year, boosting the workers' debt in two ways. First, they receive an extremely low wage for their product, and second, during the months when the agents refuse to buy, the bonded workers are unable to make payments on their loans and their interest debt rises more sharply than usual. They are also likely to have to take additional loans to cover basic expenses during this period, thus falling even further into debt. Despite the fact that they are paid on a piece-rate basis, bonded laborers are not permitted to sell their product or labor to anyone other than the agent who gave them their advance.

## *Health hazards*

The primary health hazard of gem work is damage to the vision. Dozens of facets are cut on each tiny gem, and both the cutting and polishing processes requires close and meticulous examination of the stone.[137] Eyesight deteriorates significantly within ten years, and many gem workers needing corrective eyewear after the age of twenty, usually because of progressive presbyopia (a form of farsightedness).[138]

## *Applicable law*

All agents and employers of bonded child labor in the gem industry are violating the Bonded Labour System (Abolition) Act, the Child Labour (Prohibition and Regulation) Act (regulatory provisions), and the Children (Pledging of Labour) Act. A substantial but unknown percentage of these employers are also violating the Factories Act, which applies to workshops of ten or more people when power is used in the process, as it is in gem cutting and polishing.

## SILK

The production of silk thread and the silk saris woven from that thread is historically one of India's most important industries. The saris, worn by many Indian women, range from relatively affordable basic saris to the intricate and expensive ceremonial, wedding, and *haute couture* saris. The latter are painstakingly handwoven of domestically-produced silk thread and adorned with elaborate designs woven in gold thread. Two Indian cities, Varanasi in the north and Kanchipuram in the south, are famous for their elegant silk saris. A moderate Kanchipuram silk sari sells for about two hundred U.S. dollars—more than the annual wage of India's poorest quarter, and a hefty amount for even the most solidly middle class.

---

[137] There are five distinct stages of gem production: slicing, shaping, preforming, faceting, and polishing. Each of these stages requires minute and sustained attention to detail. *Report of the Commission on Bonded Labour in Tamilnadu*, p. 75.

[138] Vidyasagar, "A Status Report....," p.13, citing eye specialist Dr. Jaiswal. According to Dr. Jaiswal, eyeglasses are not usually required by the general population until after the age of thirty-five.

India is the world's second largest producer of silk, but India only accounts for 5 percent of the global silk market.[139] This market share was still enough to generate approximately $260 million in revenues during 1995.[140] Germany, the largest consumer of Indian silk, imported DM 540 million ($231 million) in 1995.[141] The bulk of Indian silk thread and silk cloth, however, are consumed domestically.

The silk industry has been expanding rapidly over the last several years, with substantial government and international subsidies for sericulture projects and marketing schemes.[142] In 1996-97, the Indian government expects silk exports to reach an all time high of $300 million.[143] In addition to government promotion, a major funder of the silk industry is the World Bank. From 1980-89, the World Bank began active promotion of the silk industry as a means of development by loaning $54 million to support sericulture in Karnataka.[144] In 1989, the World Bank provided two more loans totaling $177 million for the National Sericulture Project of which Karnataka and Uttar Pradesh are recipients.[145] In total, the World Bank provided $231 million for the expansion of the industry from 1980-89. In 1994 and 1995, the Bank provided a $3 million loan to modernize the Karnataka silk industry and provided further assistance on a $157 million project to upgrade

---

[139] "Silk Exports May Fall 20 Percent," *Business Line*, March 7, 1996.

[140] Ibid.

[141] "Indo-German Trade Surges By 20% to DM 8.17 Billion," *Business Standard*, June 12, 1996.

[142] See Sanjay Sinha, *The Development of Indian Silk: A Wealth of Opportunities* (New Delhi: Oxford and IBH Publishing Co. Pvt. Ltd., 1990), p. 46-47, 56-59; government subsidies as of 1990 totaled $20 million annually; *The Hindu*, "Sericulture project for 7 more districts," November 21, 1995, p. 5. The article reported that World Bank funding of sericulture projects would continue and the annual production of silk was expected to more than double by end of eight-year project. "Sericulture" refers to the culture of the silkworm.

[143] "Silk Exports May Fall 20 Percent," *Business Line*, March 7, 1996.

[144] Public Interest Research Group, *The World Bank and India* (New Delhi: Public Interest Research Group, 1994), p. 81.

[145] Ibid., p. 82.

the production and quality of Indian silk.[146] The Bank has also proposed a $190 million loan for the development of agriculture in Uttar Pradesh, of which promotion of sericulture is a component.[147] The Bank believes that assisting the promotion of sericulture will create jobs, alleviate poverty, and help disadvantaged groups, as stated in a 1994 publication:

> . . . India's government decided to increase and improve India's production of raw silk to meet both domestic and export needs. The World Bank is providing financial assistance for this effort. Increasing domestic production of raw silk has the potential to create jobs, increase incomes, and reduce poverty. The Bank-supported project supports... efforts to increase the role of disadvantaged groups in silk production... Because it is land-and labor-intensive, sericulture is an ideal activity for small farmers, giving a high rate of return to both families and rural communities.[148]

By promoting these projects without placing any restrictions or monitoring requirements on the use of bonded children, the Bank has, in effect, supported a system of production which relies on bonded child labor at all stages of operation: reeling the silk fibers from the cocoons; twisting the fibers into thread; dyeing the silk; preparing the looms for weaving; weaving itself, and assisting the master weavers with the most complex work.

---

[146] "Karnataka to Have 7 Integrated Silk Growth Centres," *Business Line*, January 31, 1996; "Silk—Mixed Fare on the Cards for the Future," *Economic Times*, February 3, 1996.

[147] The World Bank, *India-UP Diversified Agriculture Support Project (DASP)*, Project Identification Number INPA35824, Proposal Date: March, 1995.

[148] The World Bank, *Working With NGOs* (Washington D.C.: The World Bank, 1994), p.5.

This report discusses two main stages of production: silk reeling and twisting and silk handlooms.[149] The rate of bondage for these child workers, who are not the children of employers, is reportedly 100 percent.[150]

It is not unusual for children as young as five to begin working in the silk industry. Some work alongside their bonded parents, assisting them as they weave fine saris. Others are contracted out to silk twisting factories or work locally as silk reelers, pulling the fine threads off the boiling cocoons. Still others are bonded to employers of relatively modest means, who may have only two looms in their houses and their own children working alongside the bonded children. All of these children earn very low wages, typically ten rupees a day or less, suffer occupational hazards and the threat of employer abuse, and are not free to leave their employer for whatever reason. They are, in the words of one researcher, "cage-birds... condemned from their very birth to be captive workers..."[151]

### Silk reeling

Karnataka, in southern India, is the country's primary silk producer. Ninety percent of India's silk thread is produced in that state, and approximately 400,000 people in Karnataka make their living from the cultivation of silkworms or the production of silk thread.[152] An estimated 100,000 of these workers are children.[153]

---

[149] There is also a significant amount of bonded child labor in the silk powerloom industry, with at least 35,000 bonded children working the powerlooms of Tamil Nadu alone. This area demands further investigation and action on the part of government authorities, but is beyond the scope of the present report.

[150] Human Rights Watch interview with researcher R. Vidyasagar, November 17, 1995, Madras; *Report of the Commission on Bonded Labour in Tamilnadu*, October 31, 1995, Madras, submitted in connection with Supreme Court Civ. Writ Petition No. 3922 of 1985, p. 73; R.K. Misra, *Preliminary Report on the Child Labour in the Saree Industry of Varanasi*, Human Rights Cell, Banaras Hindu University, Varanasi, 1995, p. 10.

[151] Misra, *Child Labour in the Saree Industry of Varanasi*, p. 3.

[152] Human Rights Watch interview with director of government cocoon market, December 7, 1995, Magadi, Karnataka.

[153] No systematic study has been undertaken on child labor in the silk industry of Karnataka. Nonetheless, a detailed study of one *Taluk* (subdivision of a district) near Bangalore found 10,000 bonded child silk workers in that *Taluk* alone. Based on this figure,

Reeling is the process by which the silk filaments are pulled off the cocoon. The cocoons are cooked in boiling water in order to loosen the sericin, a natural substance holding the filaments together. The reeler dips his or her hands into the scalding water and palpates the cocoons, judging by touch whether the fine threads of silk have loosened enough to be unwound. When they are ready, the worker finds the ends of eight to ten filaments and gently begins to reel them off. The average length of a single unbroken filament is 700 meters.[154]

More than 80 percent of silk reelers are under twenty years of age, with most of them between ten and fifteen years old.[155] As in other industries, the myth of children having natural advantages and skills is used to justify the exploitation of young girls and boys in this dangerous work. This myth is perpetuated not just by the employers of the children, but by society as a whole, including the educated elite. As one writer put it, "[m]uch of the manual work... requires skills and a delicate touch, for which the supple hands of children are regarded as more suitable."[156] The children are not permitted to use spoons instead of their hands when checking the boiling cocoons, on the theory that their hands can more easily discern when the threads are ready to reel.[157]

Human Rights Watch spoke with two boys who worked as silk reelers in the Karnataka town of Ramanagaram, India's largest cocoon market.[158] Ajad and Marukh, both ten years old, had been working in the silk industry since the age of five—Ajad for an advance of 1,000 rupees and Marukh for an advance of 5,000. According to the boys, the advances are given in order to keep the children tied to the employers and prevent them from leaving the factories. If they try to leave they are beaten. The children earn twenty rupees a day for reeling the threads off the

--------

an overall estimate of 100.000 is conservative.

[154] Sinha, *The Development of Indian Silk: A Wealth of Opportunities* (New Delhi: Oxford and IBH Publishing Co. Pvt. Ltd., 1990), p. 11.

[155] Ibid., p. 31.

[156] Ibid. at 31.

[157] Memorandum to Human Rights Watch from author Rudi Rotthier and photographer Marleen Daniels, November 1, 1995 (Rotthier/Daniels memorandum).

[158] Human Rights Watch interviews, December 6, 1995, Ramanagaram, Karnataka.

boiling cocoons, as compared to ten rupees a day for other jobs. Their work hours vary tremendously with the seasons, depending on market demand and cocoon availability.

Ajad and Marukh were initially identified by Human Rights Watch researchers as silk reelers on the basis of their hands. Their palms and fingers were white with the thick tracks of fissures, burns, and blisters.

### Silk twisting

Silk twisting (or twining) is the process whereby individual silk threads are twisted into a strong multi-ply thread. Twisting usually takes place in small factories with between fifty and a few hundred spindles. These factories utilize bonded child labor. In one *Taluk* (subdivision of a district) alone, there are about one hundred twining factories, together employing more than 8,000 children, all of them believed to be bonded.[159]

The children tend to the spindles, fitting them with thread, correcting deviations, and performing other routine tasks. Many of the factories seen by Human Rights Watch were dark and stuffy, with doors shut and windows barred, filled with the deafening racket of the clacking machines.

Advances from twining factory owners range from 2,000 to 10,000 rupees. During the first six months of their employment, children earn just two or three rupees a day, enough for a snack or, for those living far away, enough for bus fare to the factory. After this initial "training" period ends, children earn between fifty paise and two rupees an hour, depending on their age and skill. The typical work day is from 7:00 a.m. until 8:00 p.m., not including transit time to and from the factories. Child workers, who are recruited from all the villages in the area, travel an average of twelve kilometers to the factories where they work. Many children spoke to us of their walk home from work as their only pleasure of the day, a chance to relax and talk with their friends. The walk to work in the morning, on the other hand, is filled with anxiety. The work is difficult and the days long, and they face beatings and scoldings from their employers if they slow down or ask questions. The bondage in some cases is also quite tangible; a pair of Belgian investigators who visited the area in 1995 found several instances of children being locked inside the factories to prevent their exit during the frequent power outages.[160]

---

[159] Results of a 1995 survey conducted by social service organization in Magadi Taluk, rural Bangalore District, Karnataka.

[160] Rotthier/Daniels memorandum.

When they reach the age of seventeen or eighteen the children are released. As adults, they would be entitled to higher wages. Rather than pay these wages, the employers fire them and bring in a new batch of younger children to take their places.[161]

### Testimonies of Child Silk Twisters[162]

**Mylappa**, an eight-year-old boy, had been working in a silk twisting factory for three years when he was interviewed by Human Rights Watch. There are six members in his family. They are landless, do not own their own house, and have no assets. They depend on their physical labor in order to survive.

All six of them work in silk reeling and twisting. Mylappa's mother took an advance of 14,000 rupees after his father died; part of the money was used for funeral expenses, and the rest for the basic cost of living. Each of them is now working for this creditor/owner in an attempt to repay the loan.

Mylappa earns one rupee an hour and works twelve hour day. He and the other workers do not receive wages for the periods of the power shutdowns, but are nonetheless required to remain in the factory, available to do whatever odd jobs the employer might request, including domestic chores in the owner's house. Mylappa is scolded if he arrives late to work, and his legs hurt from standing all day. When he asks for a raise the owner beats him. Mylappa is unable to join another factory, where he might earn more or be better treated, because of the advance from the current employer.

Mylappa told us that his legs and hands are sometimes injured by the machine, and his fingers are frequently cut. When he is injured, the owner will not send him for medical treatment.

Mylappa walks two kilometers to work. He works until 9:00 p.m. and then walks home with his friends. He reported being happy at the end of the day because the tension is finally over. On the way to work he can not enjoy himself

---

[161] Human Rights Watch interview with social activist, December 7, 1995, rural Bangalore district.

[162] Human Rights Watch witnessed many children working in the twining factories and spoke with several of them briefly, usually in view of their employers. We were unable to gain access to the children in a setting more secure and conducive for interviews. Instead, we relied largely on information provided by a local social welfare organization. Although the particulars of these three testimonies were confirmed repeatedly by our own conversations and observations, the testimonies themselves were recorded by this organization and not by Human Rights Watch.

at all, because he is nervous about the upcoming long day and the dangers of the employer and the machines.

**Kali**, a nine-year old girl, has been working in a silk factory since her father died three years ago. Her mother accepted a 4,000 rupee advance in order to pay for the after-death rituals and also to feed her family. They have no land. Her mother works as a stone cutter.

Kali leaves home at 7:00 in the morning and returns at 9:00 in the evening; it is a two kilometer walk to the factory. Occasionally she is allowed to sit for a few minutes when the power goes out—otherwise she is on her feet for this entire fourteen hour day. She earns one and a half rupees an hour, for an average of 200 rupees a month. Her employer scolds her fiercely if she is late and beats her if she asks about her wages. She can't leave his employ until the advance is repaid, but she and her mother together do not even earn enough to cover the family's monthly expenses, much less pay back the loan.

Kali has never been to school.

**Pomabhai** is a twelve-year-old boy. Both he and his elder sister work in silk; his other two siblings are in school and his father works as a waiter in a local hotel.

When he was eight his father took a 4,500 rupee advance in order to pay for the oldest daughter's marriage; Pomabhai was taken out of school and put in the factory, and he has been working there ever since. "I want to continue my education," he says. "But first, we have to eat."

### *Work Conditions and Health Hazards of Silk Reeling and Twisting*

As a consequence of the constant immersion in scalding water, the skin on the hands of the child silk reelers becomes raw, blistered, and sometimes infected. As one team of investigators described it, "thousands of children work in these factories, with hands that seem to belong to ninety year olds."[163] In addition to the skin ailments, reelers frequently suffer from respiratory problems, caused by the constant inhaling of the sericin vapors.[164]

The workers in the silk twisting factories suffer pain in their legs and backs from standing all day without rest. Some of them develop leg deformities over the years, including bowleggedness. The boys and girls also suffer occasional injuries—mainly cuts—from the machines, particularly to their hands and fingers.

---

[163] Rotthier/Daniels memorandum.

[164] Sinha, *The Development of Indian Silk,* p. 63.

Many children mentioned injuries severe enough to warrant medical attention and prevent further work by the victims.[165]

### Employer Abuses in Silk Reeling and Twisting

Abuses common to other bonded industries are found in silk production as well: verbal abuse, including threats and harsh language; physical abuse in the form of blows for arriving late, working slowly, or annoying the employer; and physical abuse by denying the children adequate rest and recovery time.

Girl factory workers also suffer from sexual abuse at the hands of their employers. Girls are preferred by owners because they are believed to be more obedient, docile, and submissive. According to the activists and investigators in the area, girls are also frequently targeted for sexual assault by the owners inside the factories. The practice is so prevalent that it is difficult for these girls to get married when the time comes. Because of the high rate of abuse, everyone assumes that the factory girls have been "touched," that is, molested or raped by their employers. As a consequence, they are shunned as potential brides.[166]

### Silk Weaving

The greatest concentration of silk weavers is found in and around the cities of Kanchipuram, in the southern state of Tamil Nadu, and Varanasi, in the northern state of Uttar Pradesh. Both cities are famous for their fine handwoven saris. There are 50,000 to 60,000 silk handlooms in Tamil Nadu[167] and nearly 130,000 in Uttar Pradesh.[168] Silk handlooms are also found in the states of

---

[165] A researcher who undertook a detailed study of the industry reported that girls who work in the silk factories tend to have irregular and very painful menstrual periods, and may suffer other reproductive problems. Human Rights Watch interview with social activist in a village in Rural Bangalore district, Karnataka, December 7, 1995. A female leather worker interviewed in Ambur, Tamil Nadu, reported the same phenomenon in the shoe factories of that town. To Human Rights Watch's knowledge, there has been no effort by the government to investigate these or other health problems experienced by working children.

[166] Ibid.

[167] Human Rights Watch interview with researcher R. Vidyasagar, Nov. 17, 1995, Madras; Report of the Commission on Bonded Labour in Tamilnadu, Oct. 31, 1995, Madras, submitted in connection with Supreme Court Civ. Writ Petition No. 3922 of 1985, p. 76.

[168] Misra, Preliminary Report on the Child Labour, p. 8.

Karnataka (22,800), Bihar (16,000), Andhra Pradesh (15,000), West Bengal (12,800), Orissa (5,000), Assam (5,000), Madhya Pradesh (4,000), Jammu and Kashmir (1,500), and Maharashtra (225).[169]  Although this report focuses on bonded child labor in the silk handloom industries of Kanchipuram and Varanasi,[170] there is no evidence to indicate that industry practices are different in the other locales.

In Kanchipuram, 40,000 to 50,000 children work in bondage on the silk handlooms.[171] In Varanasi, approximately 85,000 children work as bonded laborers on the handlooms.[172] Most of the children work as assistants to the adult master weavers. They stretch the warps for the looms and fit the bobbins in the shuttles in preparation for the actual weaving. They then sit beside the master weavers all day long, helping to lift the warp threads and manually feed the weft threads for the intricate designs of the silk saris. Skilled children over the age of twelve may themselves work as weavers on simple, less-expensive saris.

Children commonly enter the hand weaving industry between the ages of six and nine and continuing working in that occupation their entire lives. In Varanasi, advances reportedly range from 2,000 to 5,000 rupees, while in Kanchipuram the advances are the highest of any industry, with children as young as six bringing in advances of 10,000 rupees and older children being traded for advances of up to 15,000. Sometimes whole families or sets of siblings are bonded together; this is particularly likely to occur after the death of a father, although it is common to see two-parent families in bondage as well.

Bonded silk workers interviewed by Human Rights Watch included one family of five—father, mother, daughter, and two sons—that came into bondage

---

[169]  Sinha, *Development of Indian Silk*, p. 34.

[170]  On November 24-25, 1995, Human Rights Watch interviewed forty people in four of the Kanchipuram area regarding the use of bonded child labor in the silk handloom industry. Most of those interviewed were bonded child laborers; others were parents of working children, non-bonded child workers, owners, employers, and agents. Except where otherwise noted, all information regarding the practices of the Kanchipuram silk industry was obtained during these interviews. All information regarding the practices of the Varanasi silk industry is from Misra, *Preliminary Report on the Child Labour*, except where otherwise noted.

[171]  Human Rights Watch interview with researcher R. Vidyasagar, Nov. 17, 1995, Madras, Tamil Nadu.

[172]  Misra, *Preliminary Report on the Child Labour*, p. 8.

seven years ago as the result of a 45,000 rupee loan (about $1,350). They have no idea when their servitude will end. A family of three—mother, father, and daughter—was bonded four years ago for 50,000 rupees. They also do not know how long they will be working to pay this debt. Many other bonded children worked as assistants to their own parents. Some of them had been working thirty years or more, since they themselves were young children.

### The Structure of Work

As is true of all the industries discussed in this report, the silk industry has a vertical structure. At the bottom is the child laborer, who assists the master weavers. In terms of power to control their own work and negotiate wages, the master weavers rank above the child assistants, but barely. The weavers work extremely hard for long hours and low pay—thirty to forty rupees per day is the typical wage scale. Frequently, they are themselves bonded.

The next rung up is the owner of the loom. The power and wealth of loom owners varies greatly. Silk weaving "factories" are plentiful in the Kanchipuram area. These factories may have anywhere from twenty-five to several hundred looms—the bigger the factory, the more powerful the owner, and the more likely he is to offer hefty advances in order to secure his workers. Human Rights Watch interviewed one factory owner who had four hundred looms, with one thousand employees to work them. Half of these employees were children. This man, the richest and most powerful in his village, commonly gave advances of 10,000 rupees or more, had the debtors "sign" a "contract" acknowledging this debt, and then used local police power to enforce the "contract." (See below.)

The wealthy owner of a large factory represents one end of the continuum. At the other end are rural owners who enjoy a more modest economic advantage over their neighbors and the weavers they employ. For example, one employer in a poor village had three looms in his small house. One he worked himself, and the other two were worked by bonded neighborhood children, who were secured with advances of 1,000 to 2,000 rupees each. The owner had himself worked as a child laborer on the looms of Kanchipuram, including two years with no pay. Now, with three looms and four hired workers, he is considered middle-class and views himself as a benefactor to the community. "After learning myself, I am now giving work to others," he said.

Above the loom owners is the buyer or merchant's agent. This man advances the materials and tells the owner what designs to produce. In some cases, as for example with the wealthy owner of a large number of looms, it is the owner himself who procures the materials and decides which patterns to produce. In these cases, the two roles of owner and buyer are combined into one. Poorer owners, however, are subject to the direction of the buyer or merchant's middleman. As in other industries where middlemen both advance materials and buy the finished product (see chapters on gemstones and carpets), the worker is exploited financially during both the pre- and post-production exchanges.

At the top of the hierarchy is the merchant, who may trade domestically, for export, or both. Again, the wealthier handloom factory owners may subsume this role as well.

It is the people in the top two roles—the buyers and the merchants—who truly profit from the cheap and forced labor of the bondage system. A researcher in Varanasi described the hierarchy of exploitation as follows:

> In this set up, it is the master weaver-cum-owner of the loom who is actually exploiting the child worker but he is not the ultimate beneficiary. The piece rate arrangement under which he works hardly provides his subsistence and forces him to employ the child on very low wages. The real beneficiaries of the exploitation of the child are *Mahajan* [buyer/agent] and *Gaddidar* [merchant trader] who never deal with the child worker.[173]

### The Structure of Bondage

Depending upon the wealth of the loom owner, the size of the factory, and the age and skill of the child, advances range from 1,000 to 15,000 rupees. As in other bonded industries, the purpose of the advance is to secure the child's captive labor. Repayment of the loan is not the owner's priority. To the contrary, the owner prefers that the debt remain outstanding, and the low wages paid virtually guarantee that it does.

In both Varanasi and Kanchipuram, children earn between fifty and 300 rupees monthly (two to ten rupees a day), depending on their skill and the duties they perform. Children over twelve may earn slightly more than this if they are working as weavers.

According to the Varanasi researcher, these low wages are not a function of a rational economic calculation of the employer's costs and profits, but are rather an arbitrary continuation of historic pay patterns. "An attempt was made to find out from the employers the basis adopted for the fixation of wages of child workers but no rational explanation... was forthcoming. The patterns have reproduced themselves over the years and most of the manufacturing units follow the prevalent

---

[173] Misra, *Preliminary Report on the Child Labour*, p. 11.

norms and do not... take the economics of the units into account while determining the wages. There is... an effective understanding between the employers... so that [there is] very little variation in the wage pattern."[174]

In the case of medium and large-scale loom owners, there is room for higher wages to be paid if the employers so desired. The owner of a ten-loom factory told Human Rights Watch that it takes fifteen to twenty days to weave a sari that will sell for 12,000 rupees. The owner receives 90 percent of this 12,000, while the agent receives 10 percent. Assuming the sari were woven in twenty days by a master weaver and a child helper, and assuming that the weaver earned forty rupees a day while the child earned ten, the breakdown of the earnings would be: child, 200 rupees; adult weaver, 800 rupees; agent, 1,200 rupees; and owner/employer, 9,800 rupees, less costs.

Low wages, coupled with the debt incurred by the children's parents, ensure a long period of servitude, as described in the following account:

> One cannot become a weaver before he is about 14 years of age, depending upon his ability to learn and his physical development.... Having worked at very low wages as a child worker before he matures into a weaver, he would not have the necessary capital to install his own loom and to arrange for the material to be able to work on his own. Besides, there may be the liability of an advance taken by his parents which has to be cleared. All this forces him to work on the loom owned by someone else (generally the loom-owner who employed him as a child worker) on a piece-rate basis... Thus one who starts as a child labourer has to remain a captive of the loom owner for a number of years even after becoming a weaver... the exploitation of the child worker continues even after he ceases to be a child and matures into a fulfledged weaver. While working on the loom of his previous employer-cum-creditor, his bargaining power to settle the wages remains circumscribed by his outstanding obligations to his previous employer.... The system so operates that a weaver does not become independent till he reaches 30 or 35 years of age.[175]

---

[174]  Ibid., p. 30.

[175]  Ibid., pp. 10-11.

The use of written contracts by Kanchipuram loom owners is a striking exception from the practice of most other bonded industries, where pledging agreements are entered into orally. According to a wealthy handloom factory owner and his son, a manager of the business, contracts are written for bondage agreements that involve advances of 10,000 rupees or more. They referred to these contracts as "bond papers." The parents who are turning their children (or themselves) over in exchange for the advances sign these contracts, although most of them are illiterate, cannot read the contract, and sign with a thumbprint. If a worker complains to the police or attempts to escape, the factory owner will show the police the bond paper in order to prove the debt of the worker. Of course, such contracts are void in India as a matter of law, under the Bonded Labour System (Abolition) Act and the Children (Pledging of Labour) Act. Nonetheless, the police, when contacted by the local owners, will forcibly return the runaway workers to their employers and hence to their servitude.

At the more rural level, where employers have fewer looms and offer smaller advances, written contracts are not used. Advances are given to local residents only, to reduce the risk that the children will run away. When escapes do happen or when there are other problems with enforcing the debt obligation, the employers turn to the local *panchayat* (village elders/town council) for help in resolving the dispute. The *panchayat* is supposed to enforce contracts for the pledging of child labor, fining those who have tried to escape from the employer or end the servitude without paying back all advances in full.

In both urban and rural settings, then, bonded child labor is enforced with the help of local authorities, despite the fact that the practice has been illegal for more than sixty years.

### Work Conditions in Silk Weaving: Health Hazards and Employer Abuse

Given the conditions under which they labor, it is not surprising that many children attempt to escape from bondage.[176] The work is grueling, requiring speed and precision if the child is to avoid damaging the expensive weavings. The children work eleven hours a day, six and a half days a week. Some children work even more days, depending on their employer; two young sisters near Kanchipuram

---

[176] One wealthy employer told Human Rights Watch researchers, in an interview in Kanchipuram on November 23, 1995, that he has suffered losses totaling 200,000 rupees because of children running away. While he declined to specify how many children ran away or over what period of time this loss occurred, this figure is a clear indicator of the desperate conditions and deep suffering of the bonded child laborer's life.

reported working every day of the year except for the holidays of Pongal (in January) and Diwali (in October or November).

Most silk looms are crowded together in dark, damp, and poorly-ventilated rooms or buildings. This crowded work environment encourages the spread of contagious illnesses among the child silk workers—one expert named tuberculosis and digestive disorders as "the occupational disease of the weaving community."[177] Proper physical development is inhibited by the requirement that the children sit at the looms for long stretches at a time with their legs tucked under them or hanging down below in the cold and damp recesses underneath the looms. This leads to a high prevalence of back and leg ailments, including damaged knee joints and rheumatism. Poor lighting and the constant visual strain it produces damage the eyesight. A more obvious and immediate health threat, and one frequently mentioned by the child workers themselves, is the damage to the fingers from the constant handling of the fine silk threats. Cuts are endemic and difficult to cure. A researcher in Kanchipuram reported seeing a boy with fingers so sore from cuts that he was unable to eat. Employers do not provide medical care or even first aid to injured workers, and those who are unable to work receive no wages for the day.

The children told us that they work in fear of their employers and the master weavers, who frequently scold and berate them with harsh language. This "discipline" is reinforced by occasional blows, particularly when the children make mistakes, as they inevitably do while learning the trade. More severe punishment may be meted out to recalcitrant children. The study of child silk workers in Varanasi, undertaken by the Human Rights Cell of Banaras Hindu University in Varanasi, was sparked by a news item appearing in a daily paper. The story told of a child assistant to a sari weaver who had been "beaten up by the employer and placed in iron fetters." The newspaper published a photograph of the child.[178]

As the investigators soon found, this treatment of the boy worker was completely sanctioned by his community, including his family. It appears that the boy had failed to report to work on repeated occasions. When beatings failed, the employer placed him in leg irons. This was, it seems, "an approved method of mending the ways of one who played truant from the work." No one in the

---

[177] B.N. Juyal, *Child Labour: The Twice Exploited* (Varanasi: Gandhian Institute of Studies, 1985).

[178] *Jagaran*, Dec. 14, 1994 (cited by Misra, *Preliminary Report on the Child Labour*, p. 5).

community, including the boy's parents, wanted to initiate criminal proceedings against the employer.[179]

### Applicable Domestic Law and Enforcement

#### Bonded Labour System (Abolition) Act
#### Children (Pledging of Labour) Act

All of the practices described above, in silk reeling, twisting, and weaving, constitute debt bondage and violate the Bonded Labour System (Abolition) Act and the Children (Pledging of Labour) Act. This is true even in those rare cases where children are working without advances having been taken against them; the Bonded Labour System (Abolition) Act includes within its ambit work for "nominal wages," defined by the Supreme Court as wages less than the minimum wage. As one prominent Indian legal expert put it, although there is no set minimum wage for the sari industry, the children's monthly salaries of 150 to 300 rupees "can by no stretch of the imagination be deemed as minimum wages."[180]

Despite this, and despite the widespread knowledge of the use of advances in the silk and sari industry (including, for example, news accounts like that of the boy in leg irons), there have been no known prosecutions under the Bonded Labour System (Abolition) Act, much less convictions.[181]

#### Child Labour (Prohibition and Regulation) Act

Cloth weaving is a hazardous industry as defined by the Child Labour (Prohibition and Regulation) Act, and the employment of any child under the age of fourteen in this industry is illegal. Although employment of children as silk reelers and twisters is not similarly forbidden, the conditions under which they work violate the regulatory provisions of the Child Labour (Prohibition and Regulation) Act.[182] Nonetheless, not a single prosecution or conviction is known

---

[179]  Ibid.

[180]  Misra, *Preliminary Report on the Child Labour*, p. 47.

[181]  "Thousands of persons are committing offenses under this act every year. However not one person is known to have been convicted in Varanasi." Ibid., p. 44. Nor have there been any convictions in the Kanchipuram area.

[182]  See chapter on applicable law.

to have been mounted for violations of the Child Labour (Prohibition and Regulation) Act by employers in the sari industry.[183]

### Factories Act

The Factories Act forbids the employment of children under fourteen in all factories, defined as premises employing ten or more people where power is used or twenty or more people where power is not used. Applying this definition, child labor is prohibited in all of the silk twisting factories and many of the silk weaving centers or factories. Human Rights Watch is unaware of any prosecutions under the Factories Act.

The government's failure to enforce applicable child welfare laws against violators in the silk industry is all the more disturbing in light of the government's heavy subsidies to and regulation of that industry. Up to the point where the silk is twisted, all steps of the sericulture and silk production industries are regulated by the government: a license from the state sericulture department is required in order to buy or sell cocoons, and a license, issued only after an inspection by the state, is required for all silk reeling centers.[184] In addition, the government offers extensive subsidies and incentives to businesses operating in all phases of silk production, from mulberry planting through export promotion.[185] To offer this much support to the industry while turning a blind eye to its exploitation of more than 250,000 bonded child laborers renders the state at best complicit in these criminal abuses, and at worst an active partner to them.

Local law enforcement officials, or some portion of them, are without question actively assisting the perpetration of virtual slavery upon the young silk workers. When police officers return children (or adults) to a bond master to ensure that they finish paying their "debts," they are not only failing to enforce the law, they are themselves breaking it. Whether these state-sponsored abuses are due to ignorance of the law or, as is more likely, corruption, they are the most brutal aspect of the bondage system—it not only violates the most fundamental rights of children, but uses the police power to further this violation.

---

[183] Human Rights Watch interview with North Arcot District Collector M. P. Vijaykumar, Nov. 27, 1995, Vellore, Tamil Nadu; Misra, *Preliminary Report on the Child Labour*, p. 42.

[184] Human Rights Watch interview with director of government cocoon market, Dec. 7, 1995, Magadi, Bangalore Rural District, Karnataka.

[185] Sinha, *Development of Indian Silk*, pp. 47, 57.

## LEATHER

The global leather and footwear industry has changed tremendously in the past decade, moving away from industrialized countries and into developing countries, where labor costs and production costs overall are much lower. As a result of this shift, India's leather and footwear industry has grown astronomically in the past few years, producing shoes, sporting goods, and leather apparel for both domestic consumption and export abroad. By mid-1995, the Indian leather industry had generated about $2.5 billion in revenues, of which exports accounted for $1.5 billion; footwear accounted for $257 million of these exports.[186] The leather industry anticipates a quintupling of this figure by the turn of the century.[187]

A significant portion of this growth is coming on the backs of children. Although some factories, particularly larger enterprises in the "leather belt" of Tamil Nadu, take care to engage in reputable labor practices, others are less scrupulous. Abuses of child and bonded labor laws are particularly likely to occur in the small house-based "factories" to which shoe-component production is farmed out by contractors. By employing small numbers of people, these sub-contractors escape coverage of the Factories Act; by claiming their child workers are members of their family, they escape coverage of the Child Labour (Prohibition and Regulation) Act.[188] Even when the law does apply, state negligence in enforcing it virtually guarantees that a violating employer will escape detection and prosecution.[189]

Thousands of children are making shoes in the slums of Bombay. They construct wooden heels, plastic and leather sandals, moccasin-type shoes, regular leather shoes for men, women and children, and parts of shoes that, when completed, will enter the export market. They work in tiny manufacturing units

---

[186] "By the Skin of Its Teeth - Indian Leather Industry," *Financial Express Investment Week*, August 9, 1995; "Indian Shoe Manufacturers Increased Exports Rs. 9.14 Bil in 1994-95, Compared With Rs. 5.23 Bil in 1992-93," *Reuters*, March 27, 1996.

[187] Prakash Mahtani, Chairman of the Council for Leather Exports, predicted exports valuing seven billion dollars by the year 2000. Sharika Muthu, *Times of India*, Shoe Fair Supplement, "Global Giants Stepping into Indian Shoes," Oct. 17, 1994.

[188] The Factories Act, 1948, Sec. 2(m)(i) and (ii); The Child Labour (Prohibition and Regulation) Act, 1986, Sec. 3. (The act does not apply to workshops where occupier is assisted by family).

[189] See chapter on the role of the government.

that employ three to five children each. These children, mainly boys, are as young as six or seven years old.[190] Because so little social welfare work or organizing is being done on their behalf, their exact numbers are unknown; they are estimated to number between two and twenty thousand.[191]

The boys are trafficked to Bombay from their rural villages in Rajasthan,[192] where shoe-making is a traditional cottage industry among some lower-caste communities (traditionally, Hindus have considered leather-working of any sort to be an unclean profession). They come to Bombay for ten months at a time, working every day of the month except the days of the full moon and the new moon. Their work days begin at 5:00 or 6:00 a.m. and continue until 10:00 or 11:00 p.m. They sleep at the owner's house, often a small dwelling above or behind the "factory."

The children receive no wages for these ten months of nearly constant labor. Instead, their parents receive a payment, ranging from 500 to 5,000 rupees, at the time the child is taken away. The children return to their homes during the two-month period of the monsoon. Their contracts are then renewed; the parents paid again, and the children returned to their masters in Bombay. This cycle continues for ten or fifteen years, beginning at the age of seven or so and continuing until marrying age is reached.

A contributing economic factor behind this migration is found in the shoemaking villages of Rajasthan. Rajasthan is a poor desert state. This poverty is exacerbated by the decline of the traditional shoe market in India. Once, most rural Rajasthanis wore the traditional homemade shoes fashioned by the leather-workers. These shoes, made from cow or camel hide, are sturdy, long-lasting, and simple. It takes a man two full days to make one pair. If they are to be decorated, this is done by a woman, and also takes two full days. The shoes are sold to middlemen for one hundred rupees; after subtracting the cost of materials—leather for construction and colored yarn for decoration—this works out to an average

---

[190] Based on our observations of the Bombay leather shoe industry, girl workers comprise approximately 5 percent of the child workers overall.

[191] Human Rights Watch interview with local resident and shoemaker, January 16, 1996, Bombay.

[192] A small percentage of the boys are brought in from Uttar Pradesh and other parts of Maharashtra. These children make wooden heels for shoes, while the children from Rajasthan make the leather sandals known as *chappals*. *Times of India*, "Children toil for 12 hours in chappal units," February 12, 1996.

daily wage of about twelve rupees per worker. This is a low wage even for children, and yet it is earned by adult workers—shoemaking is a poorly rewarded occupation.[193]

These low earnings have been greatly exacerbated by the advent of cheap ready-made shoes on the marketplace. These new shoes, fashioned in small factories like those in the slums of Bombay, are attractive to the poor because they are affordable (some sell for as low as one hundred rupees) but look modern and upscale. The increasing reach of impersonal commerce into rural villages is bringing competition to the traditional producer; in the case of the shoemakers of Rajasthan, this competition has been devastating. As unemployment and poverty increases, the pressure to sell their children mounts. It is a particularly perverse irony that many of these parents are now sending their sons to work in the very factories that are rendering their own shoes obsolete.[194]

The slum Human Rights Watch visited which constituted the children's worksite was a place of appalling squalor. The amount of footwear garbage—leather, plastic, and rubber—indicated a sizeable amount of production. The children do not make complete shoes, but their components. We saw children tracing heels on wooden two by fours and cutting them out with motorized saws; cutting women's leather uppers out of leather sheets; stamping brand names on the insoles of shoes and sandals; making the straps (leather, braided leather, and plastic) for sandals; gluing soles, heels, insoles, straps, and uppers together; sewing uppers to insoles on sewing machines; stamping insoles out of sheets; stamping out soles (leather, rubber, wood); and transporting finished products to wholesalers. Every process involved in the manufacture of this footwear was done by children.

*Applicable Law*

### Bonded Labour System (Abolition) Act
The bondage of these young shoemakers is structured differently from that of their bonded brothers and sisters in most other industries. Their servitude is for a specified period of time, and the amount earned—the advance given to their

---

[193] The information on Rajasthani shoemaking communities was gathered during several Human Rights Watch interviews in villages near Viratnagar, Rajasthan, Dec. 13-14, 1995.

[194] At the same time, their daughters are being forced into carpet-weaving. See chapter on carpets.

parents—is certain. Despite these differences, the situation remains one of bondage and violates both international and domestic prohibitions on bonded labor.

The Bonded Labour System (Abolition) Act applies to, among others, situations where the debtor renders his labor (or that of a dependent) to the creditor, "for a specified period or for an unspecified period, either without wages or for nominal wages."[195] Even were the advances given to the parents to be considered "wages" for the children—which is a difficult twist of logic, since the children do not see any of this money themselves—they would only be nominal wages. Spread out over the ten-month tenure of the children's work, these advances equal compensation at the rate of seven to fourteen rupees a day (equivalent to twenty-five to forty-five cents)—and this for a sixteen-hour day.

The act defines "nominal wages" as those that are less than minimum wages or, where no minimum wage has been set, less than wages normally paid for the same or similar work in the same locality.[196] The Supreme Court reiterated this definition in an early landmark case, ruling that "where a person provides labours or service to another for remuneration which is less than minimum wage, the labour or service provided by him clearly falls within the scope and ambit of the word 'forced labour'..."[197] All forms of forced labor are forbidden under the Bonded Labour System (Abolition) Act.

### Children (Pledging of Labour) Act

The agreements between the middlemen and the parents of the bonded children also violate the Children (Pledging of Labour) Act, 1933. See chapter on applicable law.

### Child Labour (Prohibition and Regulation) Act

Although the tanning process is one of the twenty-five hazardous processes of the Child Labour (Prohibition and Regulation) Act, leather working is not, and as such is not an industry in which child labor is prohibited by law. The Child Labour (Prohibition and Regulation) Act's regulations regarding the conditions of work by children do apply, however, and are violated across the

---

[195] Bonded Labour System (Abolition) Act, Sec. 2(1)(g)(I)(1).

[196] Ibid., Sec. 2(1)(I)(a) and (b). Because no minimum wages have been set by the government for children's work, the second prong of this definition applies.

[197] *People's Union for Democratic Rights v. Union of India,* (1982) 3 SCC 235, paragraphs 259-260.

board by the employer practices described above. Provisions violated include the right to an hour of rest after three hours of work; a maximum work day of six hours; a prohibition on child work before 8:00 a.m. or after 7:00 p.m.; a prohibition on overtime; a mandatory day of rest every week; and the requirement that various health and safety precautions be observed.

## Enforcement

There has been little government effort to enforce these laws. Few inspections of the shoemaking premises take place, and there have been no prosecutions of the offending middlemen and employers who recruit and utilize children under conditions of bondage. Some attempts have been made to apply the Child Labour (Prohibition and Regulation) Act, but with no success. The Labour Commissioner for the state of Maharashtra told a reporter that "[i]t is very difficult to apprehend employers under the Child Labour (Prohibition and Regulation) Act. Thakkar Bappa colony [in Bombay] was raided by our officials twice in 1987-1988. But the employers claimed that the children were their relatives. Hence, no action could be taken against them as the Child Labour (Prohibition and Regulation) Act permits child labour in home-based industries."[198] The commissioner did not offer any information regarding the failure to apply the Bonded Labour System (Abolition) Act.

## Testimonies of Child Shoemakers

Gaining access to the children working in this industry is difficult. To the knowledge of Human Rights Watch there are no organizations working with them, there are no non-formal education centers for them, no outreach programs, and no social workers investigating their conditions of work. Nor is any government intervention occurring on their behalf. Human Rights Watch interviewed several children briefly at their places of employment. All of them said that they received only two days off a month, for the new and full moons, that they received only two meals a day and no wages, and that they had never been to school. Their ages ranged from ten to thirteen years old, and their parents had received payments of 2,500 to 4,000 rupees in exchange for ten months of their sons' lives. Most of the additional information gathered came from a young man who himself works and lives as a shoemaker in these slums.

---

[198] *Times of India,* "Children toil for 12 hours in chappal units," February 12, 1996.

## AGRICULTURE

Agriculture employs far more bonded laborers, child and adult, than all industries and services together. It accounts for about 64 percent of the general working population, 85 percent of the bonded working population overall, and 52 to 87 percent of the population of bonded child laborers.[199] Conditions for bonded agricultural laborers are among the harshest to be found: work days are extremely long, payment is nominal and may consist entirely of two meals a day and a yearly set of clothing, and the work is grueling.

Agricultural bondage is the oldest form of slavery known in India: accounts of agricultural bondage date back some 1,500 years. Of all forms of bondage, agriculture is most closely linked to caste; the caste system is most deeply entrenched in rural areas. Landlords are high caste, small landowners are of lower castes, and the landless and bonded laborers are primarily the Dalits ("the oppressed").[200] In rural areas, the master-slave relationship between the castes is not confined to land but permeates every aspect of village life.

"Untouchability" was abolished in 1950 when India adopted its constitution, and discrimination against "untouchables" was made a criminal offense under the 1955 Untouchability (Offences) Act. Nevertheless, discrimination against Dalits is pervasive throughout rural India. Dalits are not

---

[199] According to the Ministry of Labour, 84.98 percent of child labor is in agriculture. Ministry of Labour, Government of India, "Children and Work," produced for Workshop of District Collectors/District Heads on "Elimination of Child Labour in Hazardous Occupation," New Delhi, September 13-14, 1995, p. 3. For statistics on bonded child laborers, see Burra, *Born to Work...*, pp. 32-33, the range is so great because no definitive study has been undertaken to determine the number of bonded child laborers in agriculture. The 85 percent of all bonded laborers was confirmed by Anti-Slavery International in a telephone interview with Human Rights Watch on August 14, 1996; but like other statistics on bonded and child labor, no comprehensive survey has been taken to document this.

[200] Dalit groups have largely rejected the terms "untouchable" and "harijan" (children of God) to describe their communities. They are also referred to as "scheduled castes," a term which like "scheduled tribes" refers to groups designated on a schedule attached to the Indian Constitution as entitled to special consideration, including some quotas for educational and career opportunities, in recognition of their historically disadvantaged status. Many, if not the majority of India's bonded laborers are members of the Dalit communities, or are "scheduled tribes"—indigenous tribal people, also known as *adivasi*. However, in some industries, Dalits occupy positions other than bonded laborers. In the silk industry, for example, some loom-owners and weavers are also Dalits.

allowed to live in the same part of a village as higher caste landlords; Dalit neighborhoods are clearly demarcated from those of higher caste landowners. In addition to their geographic separation, there is a qualitative difference in their homes. Landlords predominantly live in concrete, one- or two-story houses and Dalit homes are generally thatch or mud huts or similar small dwellings. Because Dalits are prohibited from drinking the same water as higher caste villagers, they must use a separate water pump. If it breaks or otherwise malfunctions, the higher caste villagers frequently refuse to share water with the Dalits, leaving them to search for water elsewhere. Higher caste villagers will not eat with Dalits. For example, in village tea stalls or hotels, if Dalits are allowed to eat with higher castes, they are prohibited from using the same dishes as higher castes. Dalits are required to clean the village temples, but are not allowed to use them. Some Dalits are forced to do many caste-based jobs. Because they are considered "unclean," some Dalits are required to remove dead animals from the village.

Violence against Dalits is extremely common as well. Human rights groups in India have documented widespread abuses including murder, rape and other forms of violence and harassment at the hands of higher castes. In many cases, police and other government officials, many of whom belong to higher castes, have been acquiescent or even active participants in these crimes.[201]

When Dalits try to exercise their rights or resist their ongoing mistreatment, they are faced with extremely hostile, and sometimes brutal resistance by the higher caste villagers. One of the most common methods that higher caste villagers have used to quell Dalit resistance is the "social boycott." Because Dalits have been subjected to such extreme subjugation by higher caste villagers, their lives are largely dependent on the income provided by higher caste villagers. Consequently, when Dalits resist this oppression, higher caste villagers will respond by completely boycotting the Dalit community, leaving the Dalits unable to work. Higher caste villagers have attempted to literally starve the Dalits into submission.

The belief in the lower castes' inherent inferiority is tenacious and widespread, particularly in rural India. Castism is frequently cited by academics and activists as a factor in the state's failure to bring the bonded labor system to an end. Caste-based non-enforcement of the law is most serious at the local level. In many cases, government officials charged with enforcing the Bonded Labour System (Abolition) Act belong to the higher castes and are unwilling to take action against landowners and employers who are violating the act. Furthermore,

---

[201] See for example, A.R. Desai, ed. *Repression and Resistance in India*, (Bombay: Popular Prakashan Private Ltd., 1990).

widespread societal acceptance of the inequities of the caste system means that there is little external pressure on the bureaucrats to fulfill their legal duty *vis a vis* the bonded laborers. However, Dalit political leaders who have come to power in greater numbers in the 1990s have also failed to address the problems of bonded labor.

The area in which we interviewed children is known as Anekal Taluk. It is in the state of Karnataka and about fifty kilometers southeast of Bangalore, India's fifth most populous city and often referred to as India's "Silicon Valley." Anekal Taluk falls within the Bangalore Urban District and is comprised of 298 villages. The organization that works here has provided a detailed profile of 786 bonded laborers, and the incidence of bonded labor in Anekal Taluk is a case study of government negligence.

### Testimonies of Children in Anekal Taluk

Human Rights Watch interviewed several adults and children working as bonded laborers in two villages of Anekal Taluk.[202]

**Kumaravel**, a twelve-year-old boy, has been working for the master for four years. In 1995 he received 3,000 rupees; the year before that, 2,000 rupees. He works from 6:00 a.m. until 8:30 p.m., watering the land, washing the house, herding the cattle—whatever the master wants. Sometimes he is required to stay at the master's house overnight for additional work. Kumaravel works every day of the year. His effective daily wage is just over eight rupees a day. He himself never sees this money, which is given to his father once a year.

**Shankar**, an eleven-year-old boy, receives 3,000 rupees a year. He works 365 days a year, from 6:00 a.m. until 10:00 p.m. His effective hourly wage is fifty paise: half a rupee, or about a penny and a half in U.S. currency. Shankar's father, also an agricultural laborer, took the money in order to meet his family's basic needs.

**Sanjeev**, also eleven, has been working for the landlord for the last two years for a yearly wage of 2,200 rupees. He works 365 days a year, from 5:00 a.m. until 9:00 or 10:00 p.m. He tends animals and works with the crops in the field. "I do not like work; it is hard and there is no time limit. When I'm sick, the master won't let me stay home. If I try to take time off he will scold me and beat me and take me back to the fields. Sometimes he beats me because he says I am working slowly." Sanjeev has never been to school.

---

[202] All interviews by Human Rights Watch, December 9, 1995, Anekal Taluk, Bangalore Rural District.

**Rama**, a fourteen-year-old boy, earns 1,000 rupees a year. Like the others, he works every day of the year, from 5:00 a.m. to 10:00 p.m. He considers his landlord good, because he gives Rama two meals a day. Nonetheless, the master will make him work even if he is sick. Rama's effective daily wage is 2.7 rupees a day—less than one-tenth of the minimum wage.

**Rupali**, a fourteen-year-old girl, has been working in bondage for the past five years. She earns 1,500 rupees a year and works from 5:00 a.m. until 10:00 p.m., every day of the year. The master treats her badly, beats her and yells and curses at her. If she is sick, her mother must pay for treatment and then send her right back to work.

**Magala** is the nine-year-old sister of Rupali. She was pledged this year for 1,000 rupees. Like her older sister, she works from before dawn until after dark, doing whatever the master requires of her. The mother of the two girls is a widow, and blind. She depends on the advances she gets for her daughters in order to support her family.

### A Profile of Bonded Labor in Anekal Taluk

In 1988, Father Kiran Kamal Prasad, with the help of Dalit youths in the villages of Anekal Taluk, began a two-year survey of the incidence of bonded labor in the Taluk. The practice of bonded labor is colloquially known as *jeeta* and is described by Prasad as follows:

> Generally a bonded labourer is one who has to work for the master for the loan he has taken from him. He may work in his house, or in his field or in any other way. He may work for the master only to repay interest of the loan or to give back the principal itself. If the loan is a big sum, then he may have to work only for the interest. He may repay the loan by coming to an understanding regarding the yearly or monthly sum that can be deducted from the loan in consideration of the work he has put in. But normally, since he and his other family members have no other means of livelihood, he is forced to take extra loans during the course of the year to look after the day to day needs of his dependents. Thus the original loan may continue to remain as it is or it may go on accumulating. If we take the yearly or monthly sum that is agreed to be deducted for the loan, we find that it does not even come to one-fourth or one-third of the prevalent daily wages, leave alone the minimum wages, fixed by law... During certain occasions in their life [sic], the

very poor families in villages are in need of a larger sum than that which can be procured from their regular resources. The larger sum can only be procured from a wealthy person in exchange for labour to be provided by himself or one or some of his dependents, whether his wife or children or brother or parents. Marriage in a family, grave illness or even the day-to-day needs force one to have recourse to take a loan. The only security by which he can take that loan is a promise to provide his or his dependents' labour. If he is a very small or small farmer, he may even mortgage his land, which he may not be able to recover at all.[203]

On March 12, 1991, Prasad published the results of the survey.[204] It found a total of 786 bonded laborers in 120 out of 298 villages. The survey documented the caste of 731 out of the 786 people and found 690 were Dalits (Scheduled Castes), twenty-one belonged to other lower castes, eleven were dominant castes, and nine were Scheduled Tribes. Nineteen of the 786 bonded laborers were women.

The age was recorded for 727 bonded laborers. There were 147 bonded laborers aged eleven to fifteen, and thirty-five bonded children were below the age of ten. Over 300 of the bonded laborers were below the age of twenty.

The survey was able to identify who took the loan in 655 cases. In the case of children, 305 were pledged by their fathers and thirty-one children were pledged by their mothers. In 279 cases, the loan was taken by the adult bonded laborers themselves. The remaining forty bonded laborers were pledged by other members of the family including elder brothers, grandfathers, uncles, and fathers-in-law. In four cases women had been pledged by their husbands. The study found that the 786 bonded laborers belonged to 719 families.

In 691 of the 786 cases a yearly advance was given, with most of the loans under 2,000 rupees [$57.14]. The most common reason cited for taking the advance and entering into debt-bondage was to meet normal subsistence expenditures.

The families of the bonded laborers were analyzed as well, confirming the survey's findings that subsistence was the overwhelming reason for bondage. In

---

[203] Kiran Kamal Prasad, "Bonded Labour in Anekal Taluk, Bangalore Urban District, Karnataka" (Guddhati village: Self published, March 12, 1991), p.4.

[204] Ibid.

addition, the profile indicated that rural underemployment, and not specifically unemployment, was a major factor in forcing family members into bondage.

The sources of family income were reported for 662 of the 719 families. Only 10 families (1.5 percent) lived solely off the advance. The overwhelming majority of families (85.9 percent or 569 families) were also involved in daily wage labor and agricultural (non-bonded) labor. In general, 98.5 percent of families were working while also having family members bonded.

The problems of rural unemployment and underemployment are recognized as reasons that exacerbate poverty by the Indian government:

> Rural poverty is inextricably linked with low rural productivity and unemployment, including underemployment...It is estimated that in 1987-88 the rate of unemployment was only 3 percent and inclusive of the underemployed, it was around 5 percent...[P]overty for the same year was estimated to be 30 percent. This demonstrates that even though a large proportion of the rural population was 'working' it was difficult for them to eke out a living even at subsistence levels from it [work].[205]

### A Pattern of Government Negligence
In addition to conducting a detailed survey on the incidence of bonded labor, the surveyors assisted 656 bonded laborers in making applications to the district collector for their identification, release, and rehabilitation. The district collector identified only 192 as bonded laborers and earmarked 1.2 million rupees [$34,286] for their rehabilitation in 1991.[206] Prasad reported that by 1994, "not a single paise [one-hundredth of a rupee] reached the hands of the people concerned." The organization of bonded laborers then filed a writ petition with the High Court of Karnataka asking for the disbursement of funds. On the orders of the court, fifteen of the 192 bonded laborers were acknowledged by the court and about 100,000 rupees [$2,941] were released for their rehabilitation.[207]

---

[205] Government of India, *8th Five Year Plan: 1992-1997* (New Delhi: Cosmos Bookhive (P) Ltd., 1992), pp. 64-65.

[206] Kiran Kamal Prasad, "Bonded Labour in Karnataka," (Bangalore: Self published, 1995), p. 4.

[207] Ibid.

In 1993, Prasad formed a voluntary organization known as JEEVIKA, and with the help of Dalit groups, set out to identify bonded laborers throughout the state of Karnataka and submit petitions to the district collectors for rehabilitation on their behalf. By 1995, the organization had identified 18,139 bonded laborers and had submitted petitions for the rehabilitation of 16,814. The remaining 1,325 were still waiting to submit petitions.[208] When we interviewed Prasad on December 9, 1995, he informed us that the state had done nothing about the petitions.

JEEVIKA also conducted an investigation into the statistics the state government submitted to the Ministry of Labour regarding their compliance with the identification, release, and rehabilitation of bonded laborers. They found that from 1976 to 1979, the state claimed to have identified 62,389 bonded laborers. By 1992, this number had risen to 65,255, meaning that only 2,866 bonded laborers had been identified from 1979-1992.[209] They concluded:

1. The Government did not really identify the fresh cases of bonded labour after the end of 1979.
2. Even those who were identified before 1979 were from southern, developed districts. If the northern eight districts are very backward compared to the southern ones, one would presume the incidence of bonded labour to be quite high there. But the number of bonded labourers identified by the government does not mirror this fact. This means the process of identification in northern Karnataka was not adequate, and many bonded laborers have been left out without being released and rehabilitated.[210]

JEEVIKA also reported that the Karnataka government had identified and rehabilitated more bonded laborers than any other state, but that the amount of rehabilitation assistance was still inadequate and that there were many instances of many rehabilitated bonded laborers falling back into bondage.[211] The method used

---

[208]  Ibid.

[209]  Ministry of Labour statistics on bonded labour are cumulative totals. For a further discussion of these statistics and their methodology, see below.

[210]  Kiran Kamal Prasad, "Bonded Labour...", p. 3.

[211]  Ibid, p. 2.

by the state to calculate the number of bonded laborers was also seriously flawed, a problem described more fully in Chapter VI.

*Applicable Law*

### Bonded Labour System (Abolition) Act
The Bonded Labour System (Abolition) Act, 1976, specifically classifies the *Jeeta* system as a form of bonded labor in Section 2(b) of the act.

## HANDWOVEN WOOL CARPETS
The Indian carpet industry is notorious for its exploitation of child workers. Reports of severe abuse have been surfacing from the northern Indian "carpet-belt" since the mid-1980s. Despite the industry's claims that only small numbers of children work the carpet looms, and these under good conditions, frequent reports by journalists, academics, government commissions, and child welfare specialists continue to provide the dark details of bondage and savage mistreatment doled out by many carpet manufacturers.

On January 26, 1996, a New Delhi newspaper reported on the rescue of twenty-three bonded laborers by the Bonded Labor Liberation Front, one of the leading social activist organizations working on this issue. The children reported that they were forced to knot carpets eighteen hours a day and were beaten if they fell asleep or complained. They were given two poor meals a day, but never enough to satisfy them, "because if we ate to our fill we would feel sleepy." One of the boys was lashed with a whip; another hit so hard with a metal tool that he had to have the gash stitched closed; a third was burned with cigarettes when he asked about his parents. The news account ends with the boys' desires for the future, reporting that "[a]ll the younger boys want to be policemen, since they believe no one can hurt a policeman."[212] News stories such as this appear frequently.

There are 300,000 children working to produce India's fine carpets.[213] Ninety percent of these children, or about 270,000, are bonded laborers.[214] In the carpet belt of Uttar Pradesh, where most of India's carpets are woven, the vast

---

[212] "23 Children Rescued from Bondage," *The Statesman*, January 26, 1996.

[213] Pradeep Mehta, "Cashing in on Child Labor."

[214] Ela Dutt, "Rug Firms With No Child Labor Need Help," *India Abroad*, February 3, 1995.

majority of the workers are low-caste Hindu boys.  The number of girls in their ranks is increasing, however, as more children are brought in from Nepal[215] or recruited to work in other states (see "Rajasthan," below).

Built on the backs of these children, the carpet industry is one of India's most lucrative.  Carpet exports totaled more than half a billion dollars in 1994 and reached $650 million in 1995.[216]  Germany and the United States are the two largest importers of Indian carpets, accounting for about 73 percent of the export market.  Britain, Japan, and other industrialized countries also import significant amounts of the carpets.  Other major importers Indian carpets are Switzerland, Canada, Japan, Sweden, Australia, France, and Italy.[217]

India's carpet industrialists claim to be suffering from "the negative propaganda" of Indian and international nongovernmental organizations, who have been raising the issue of abusive child labor practices for several years.[218]  To date, however, the growing international awareness of the carpet industry's abuse of children has had little effect on carpet exports and earnings.  The industry, which already accounts for 2.5 percent[219] of India's total annual exports, experienced a growth rate of 11 percent in 1994—a fall from previous years but nonetheless

---

[215] See Hamish McDonald "Boys of bondage:  Child labour, though banned, is rampant," *Far Eastern Economic Review*, July 9, 1992, p. 19 (with arrival of Nepali children, including girls, reports of sexual abuse and rape increasing).

[216] "Mirzapur Carpets - Taking Exports to a New High," *Economic Times*, June 10, 1996.

[217] Since 1994, the carpet industry has been experiencing a decline in terms of global market share.  It declined to a 17 percent share of the global market in 1995, from 21 percent in 1994.  Most reports attribute this to increased competition from China and Iran.  "Hand-Knotted Carpet Units Losing Out to China, Iran," *Financial Express*, March 12, 1996; "Mirzapur Carpets - Taking Exports to a New High," *Economic Times*, June 10, 1996.

[218] "Steps taken to Curb Child Labour in Carpet Industry," *Times of India*, December 11, 1995.

[219] India's total exports in 1995 were $26.2 billion; carpet exports were valued at $650 million, or about 2.5 percent of the total exports.

robust.[220]    There are currently more than 2,000 carpet exporters in India, representing a one hundred-fold increase in less than two decades.[221]

### Mirzapur-Bhadohi:  "The Carpet-Belt"
    Approximately 90 percent of India's handwoven wool carpets are produced in the "carpet belt" of Uttar Pradesh.[222] Centered around the two towns of Mirzapur and Bhadohi, the carpet belt includes about 2,000 villages.[223] Seventy-five percent of the carpet-makers in this region are children.[224]

### Trafficking of Children
    Three main types of child laborers work in the carpet belt:  migrant bonded labor, local bonded labor, and wage earners. The worst conditions and the most severe bondage are inflicted on the migrant children, most of whom are trafficked to the carpet belt from the desperately poor state of Bihar.[225]  Some are lured in with agents' promises to their parents that the boys will receive good wages and enjoy a bright future.  Others, estimated to number in the tens of thousands, are kidnapped into bondage through force or trickery.  Anti-Slavery International, for example, reported that twenty-seven boys between the ages of five and twelve were kidnapped by their local barber, who took them in with the ruse that he was going to take them to the movies, so long as they kept it secret

---

[220] "Steps taken to Curb Child Labour in Carpet Industry."

[221]  Edward A. Gargan, "Bound to Looms by Poverty and Fear, Boys in India Make a Few Men Rich," *New York Times*, July 9, 1992.

[222]  "Mirzapur Carpets - Taking Exports to a New High."

[223]  Molly Moore, "Factories of Children: Youth Labor Force Growing in Asia to Meet Export Demand, Help Families," *Washington Post*, May 21, 1995. Although the highest concentration of carpet villages is in Mirzapur district, carpet manufacturing is also a dominant industry in the neighboring districts of Allahabad, Varanasi, and Jaunpur.

[224]  Neera Burra, *Born to Work*, p. xxii.

[225]  According to one 1995 report, carpet manufacturers have found a new way to exploit the poverty of the Bihar inhabitants:  in addition to bringing Bihar children into bondage in the carpet belt, manufacturers are beginning to bring bondage to the children, setting up hundreds of looms in the poorest districts of Bihar. See "Ex-child labourers make a fresh start," *Times of India*, July 31, 1995.

from their parents. He then sold them into slavery in a remote village of another state.[226]

Migrant child labor is extremely prevalent. Of the 300,000 children producing carpets in India, an estimated 10 to 20 percent were trafficked in to carpet-producing areas by agents. The majority of these children are forced to work several years for their bond-masters.

One systematic study found that many of the migrant children are subjected to appalling conditions:

> [They are] forced to work for long hours under inhuman conditions for no wages or nominal wages. Some of them are definitely being ill-treated, beaten, tortured, abused, branded, kept half fed, half clad, without facilities or safe drinking water, medicine, or rest, and are not allowed to move freely or change their employer.... . Four children complained that they were tied with hands folded to the legs and slung on to a jackfruit tree, then dropped on to the ground several times by pulling the rope upwards and then loosening it suddenly...[227]

In addition, the migrant child laborers are usually made to sleep in the loom shed or in other cold and cramped environments. Their food allotment is notoriously inadequate. The local bonded children may not earn higher wages, but at least they are able to sleep and eat at home.

### Structure of the Industry

Like silk, the carpet industry has a vertical structure, with importers, exporters and manufacturers (often the same person or company) at the top and, far below them, the child carpet weavers and master weavers at the bottom. In between are an average of four or five layers of subcontractors, intermediaries and agents.

---

[226] Anti-Slavery International (ASI), "Slavery Today in India," Factsheet B, July 1994. According to ASI, 10,000 boys have been kidnapped from the boys' district (Chichoria, Bihar) alone.

[227] Prem Bhai, "The Working Conditions of the Child Weaver in the Carpet Units of Mirzapur and Summary of Findings," Law Relating to Employment of Children, 1985, p. 146.

Four categories of agents work to procure fresh child labor for the manufacturers: those who live in the carpet belt and recruit children to work their own looms; those who live in the carpet belt and supply children to loom owners; agents who live elsewhere but establish ties to the carpet belt loom owners and traffic in children from their own districts; and local agents who assist outside agents by informing them which families might be vulnerable, and encouraging those families to give up their children to the carpet industry. A study conducted in Mirzapur district found that 85 percent of all bonded children are brought into bondage through the intervention of agents; only 15 percent were sold directly to an employer by a parent or guardian.[228]

The vast majority of handwoven carpet production—about 95 percent—occurs on a small cottage industry basis. Most loom owners own between one and fifty looms; of these, the majority have just a few looms and employ a handful of children to work them. These owners are not wealthy —more often, they are not even middle class, and their precarious financial state makes them feel they have no choice but to employ bonded child labor.

At the other end of the spectrum are the carpet manufacturers who own 10,000 looms or more. Some of these looms may be located together in big weaving factories, while others are scattered about in individual houses in rural villages. Under these arrangements, the loom owner may not even know exactly where all his looms are, much less visit them on a regular basis. This kind of carpet industrialist relies on a hierarchy of managers and subcontractors to get his carpets produced. As will be seen, this distancing of the owner from the actual production process renders legal accountability extremely difficult to enforce, as it is nearly impossible to trace the connection between local looms and the responsible manufacturer or exporter.

### Structure of Bondage

In the carpet belt as in Rajasthan (see below), most bonded child carpet-weavers are paid per carpet rather than a daily wage. In practice, average earnings work out to between one and ten rupees a day. Many young and recently bonded children earn no wages for several months, however, during what the employer claims to be a training period. Nor do the average earnings apply to the

---

[228] Shamshad Khan, "Migrant Child Labour in the Carpet Industry of Mirzapur-Bhadohi," (undated).

unaccompanied child workers. These children may live where they work and receive no wages, "earning" only two poor meals a day.[229]

Advances to bonded child laborers in the carpet belt range from 500 to 3,000 rupees. Although this amount theoretically can be paid off gradually by the child worker, the low wages paid virtually guarantee the impossibility of repayment and thus the long-term servitude of the child. At other times, children receive zero wages, on the grounds that all earnings are being applied toward liquidation of the debt. As in other industries, the vagueness of terms and the power advantage of the employer mean that children end up effectively repaying their debts several times over, and still are not released.

**Santosh**, a nine-year-old boy, worked as a carpet weaver for one year.[230] He worked for a local loom owner in exchange for a 500 rupee advance to Santosh's father, an illiterate and landless agricultural laborer. Santosh was never paid a single rupee, as the loom owner claimed to be deducting the wages against the debt. Even if his labor were only valued at the abysmally low rate of one and a half rupees a day (less than 20 percent of what other bonded children earn, which is itself less than 30 percent of minimum wage), Santosh's debt should have been extinguished within a year. It was not. Instead, Santosh was freed by a local social activist organization, incurring the wrath of his employer in the process.

**Das**, ten years old, worked knotting carpets for one year. He was given one or two rupees on festival days but was otherwise unpaid, on the theory that this year was a "training period."

**Imran**, sixteen, worked on the carpet looms from the age of seven until he was eleven. He was originally taken in for a 2,000 rupee advance. For his first year of work, he received no wages. During his last three years of work, he received an average of two to four rupees a day. The rest of the wages to which he was entitled were ostensibly withheld for payment of the original loan.

**Shivalinga**, a thirteen-year-old boy, stopped working last year with the support of a regional children's rights group. He had begun working at the age of nine, when his father, a landless agricultural laborer, took a 2,000 rupee advance against his son. Shivalinga was paid just twenty-five to fifty rupees upon the

---

[229] A detailed 1984 study found that approximately 50 percent of migrant child weavers were paid only in food; another 40 percent of them received only one or two rupees per day. Prem Bhai, "Working Conditions of the Child Weaver..." p. 151.

[230] Except where otherwise noted, all child testimonials from the carpet belt are drawn from Human Rights Watch interviews, December 19, 1995, in several rural villages of Mirzapur district, Uttar Pradesh.

completion of each rug—the equivalent of about one rupee per day. Had Shivalinga been paid at the rate of just ten rupees a day (which is far below minimum wage and would itself constitute proof of a bonded labor relationship), he could have paid off the original loan in eight months and, in the remaining two-plus years of his employment, earned another 7,000 rupees. Shivalinga's former employer, however, claims he is still owed the 2,000 rupee advance. The employer constantly harasses Shivalinga's father, telling him to either pay back the money or remove Shivalinga from school and send him back to the loom.

The above testimonies are from local bonded laborers, many of whose fathers are also bonded (primarily in agriculture). Migrant bonded child laborers fare even worse at the hands of their employers. Although Human Rights Watch was unable to speak with any migrant children directly, their plight has been well-documented in various reports.[231]

### Conditions of Work and Health Hazards

Children work an average of ten to fourteen hours a day, six and a half or seven days a week. Again, this frequently does not apply to the trafficked migrant children, who report being forced to work as long as sixteen or even eighteen hours on a daily basis.[232] The loom sheds are often poorly ventilated, poorly lighted, and cramped.

The long days spent in cramped positions damage the children's backs and legs, causing backaches and severe joint pain. Many of the children suffer from scabies, skin ulcers and other dermatological diseases, a result of the close and crowded conditions and the constant exposure to wool. Respiratory illnesses are rampant and eye damage is common, as are intestinal disorders. The children are also particularly vulnerable to tuberculosis and other lung diseases, which are caused and aggravated by the constant inhalation of tiny wool fibers.[233]

---

[231] See especially Prem Bhai, "The Working Conditions of the Child Weaver in the Carpet Units of Mirzapur and Summary of Findings," *Law Relating to Employment of Children*, 1985.

[232] See, e.g., "Ex-Child Labourers make a Fresh Start," *Times of India*, July 31, 1995.

[233] Information on health risks from Human Rights Watch interviews in Mirzapur district, Uttar Pradesh, and Jaipur district, Rajasthan; also McDonald, "Boys of bondage....," July 9, 1992, p. 18; Shamshad Khan, "Improvement in Health, Hygiene and Nutritional Status of Child Labour in Carpet Industry: Experience of CREDA," February 26, 1990.

Work-caused cuts and wounds are endemic and frequently become infected. When cuts occur, the loom-owners will "treat" the wounds so that the children can continue working without dripping blood on the carpets. This "treatment" consists of scraping the sulphur from match heads into the cuts and then lighting them on fire, thereby sealing the wound.

> By the time the youngsters reach their mid-teens, their fingers and hands often are badly damaged from the cuts and nicks of the knives and strings used in knotting, their eyesight has grown weak from long hours of tedious work in dark rooms, and their growth often is stunted by years of sitting in uncomfortable, hunched positions at the looms.[234]

In addition to their long hours on the loom, migrant child laborers are always subject to the demands of their master, often forced to work for the master around his house or in the field, performing whatever jobs he demands of them.[235]

### Employer Abuses

As in other industries, employers tend to treat the bonded child laborers harshly. One study of child weavers found that 71 percent reported being beaten for mistakes in weaving, and beaten even more severely if they asked for their wages or tried to escape.[236] The following comments from Munni, a nine-year-old former carpet weaver, were echoed by the majority of children speaking to Human Rights Watch.

> I got beaten if I arrived late or if I made a mistake; he was constantly abusing me. He hit me on the back and on my hand. I worked with three other children, and he hit them also. If I did not go to work, he would come to my house and catch me and beat me.

---

[234] Molly Moore, "Factories of Children: Youth Labor Force Growing in Asia to Meet Export Demand, Help Families," *Washington Post Foreign Service*, May 21, 1995.

[235] "19 Children Rescued from Bonded Labour," *Indian Express*, Nov. 9, 1995.

[236] Bhai, "The Working Conditions of the Child Weaver...", p. 151.

As mentioned, the migrant children suffer the worst abuses, with numerous reports of them being hit, tied up in trees, half-starved, and otherwise punished. Dozens of children taken to the looms of the carpet belt have later been reported missing, sold, or dead.[237]

> Tasleem, a seven-year-old with eyes that still shine in a hollow, emaciated face, longs to return to Bihar, her home. "Once when I cried for my mother, the mill owner hit me with a steel rod," she recalls.[238]

Ninety-five percent of the carpet workers in the carpet belt are boys, and sexual abuse is not a common complaint. As girls begin to enter this workforce in larger numbers, however, reports of such abuse are surfacing.[239]

### Rajasthan

Human Rights Watch visited several villages in the area of Viratnagar, in the Jaipur district of the state of Rajasthan. The inhabitants of these villages belonged to three main castes: Raigar, Rajput, and Jat. Raigar is a low caste and one of the scheduled castes; all of the carpet weavers in these villages belong to the Raigar caste. Rajput and Jat are higher castes; all of the local landholders were members of these two castes. The Raigars are traditional shoemakers, a profession considered unclean by traditional Hindus. Some of the Raigar members work as agricultural laborers for the Rajputs and Jats, but virtually none of the Raigars own any land themselves.

The carpet industry is a relatively new arrival to the rural areas of Rajasthan, beginning its encroachment just five years ago from its traditional base in the carpet-belt of Uttar Pradesh. The carpet industry's incursion into these Rajasthani villages is part of its continuing decentralization, and may be a reaction to increasing international condemnation and scrutiny of the industry's horrendous labor practices. By contracting workers on an individual basis in tiny and remote villages, the carpet manufacturers make it most difficult to hold them accountable for violations of labor laws and other protective legislation.

---

[237] Ibid., p. 152.

[238] Pradeep Mehta, "Cashing in on Child Labor."

[239] See McDonald, "Boys of Bondage...," p. 19.

The low-caste Rajasthani villagers, for their part, are vulnerable to the seduction of the carpet middleman, with his offers of cash advances and promises of a reliable career in carpet-weaving. The shoemaking that has traditionally supported these villagers is in sharp decline in today's quickly-modernizing Indian market. Those who continue to practice the ancient art have seen their earnings decline drastically in real terms in the past decade, as more and more Indians buy mass-produced shoes. A Raigar shoemaker earns only about twelve rupees per day of work—roughly a third of the average minimum wage.[240] Agricultural labor, when available, pays no better.

As a result of this worsening poverty, these villagers' children are increasingly pressed into bondage. As discussed in the chapter on leather, most of the bonded boy laborers working in the shoe industry of Bombay are from rural Rajasthan. The girl children, meanwhile, are being recruited in ever-greater numbers into the carpet industry.[241]

According to one village chief, 250 villages in the neighboring districts of Jaipur and Alwar have been completely diverted into the carpet industry since 1991. "The carpet middleman comes to the villages from Jaipur. We have a road into our village, and sometimes their vehicles come out for two hours or more, looking for new workers."[242] The middlemen form debt obligations with the rural would-be weavers by loaning them money to buy a loom and by advancing them the necessary raw materials. During the several months it takes to learn to weave, the workers earn nothing. After completing a carpet they return it to the same middleman who brought them into the industry, provided them with the wool yarn, and told them what design to produce. In this way, as in other industries (see chapters on gemstones and silk), the middleman takes a cut out of both sides of production, taking advantage of the worker's isolation and ignorance and paying only a fraction of what the labor is truly worth.

---

[240] See chapter on leather for a more detailed discussion of the Rajasthani shoemaking communities.

[241] Approximately 80 percent of the child carpet-makers in Rajasthan are female (Human Rights Watch interview with social activist, December 14, 1995, Viratnagar). This is quite different from the pattern in the Uttar Pradesh carpet belt, where 95 percent of the carpet-makers are male.

[242] Human Rights Watch interview, December 13, 1995, village near Viratnagar, Jaipur district, Rajasthan.

The adults who spoke to Human Rights Watch, mostly men, condemned the use of their children by the carpet industry. Shoemakers in the villages offered the following comments, to the unanimous assent of their listening neighbors.

> Carpet weaving gives them no support in their lives. The children weaving carpets are not in school—they get no education. Their health is destroyed. Their life is dead, once they go into carpet.

> Children who go into the carpet industry are treated like animals. Life is life, you cannot get it back once it is gone. Selling labour is not worth giving up one's life.

> Carpet-making is a very dirty profession: the wool burns in their mouths and eyes, the small children are bent over all day working, and they suffer many diseases—silicosis, tuberculosis. It is miserable. These children should be in school.

> Before the carpets came, all the children played games—they helped in the houses and with the shoes, but they also played.... Now, what can I do? I am very poor, so my two girls must both work in carpet. I don't like it, but I don't know what else we can do.

Carpet looms are everywhere in these small villages: standing under the awnings of small thatched houses, in dusty courtyards where the scrawny chickens peck, and tucked inside dark mud-walled houses. Most of the carpet weavers are girls and women, who begin their weaving days after taking care of the most pressing household work.

Twelve-year-old **Shantana** works on the carpet loom outside her house from 9:00 a.m. until 6:00 p.m.. She works seven days a week, with an occasional day off when necessary for household work or when she is ill. Shantana has been weaving on the loom since she was eight, when she was taken out of school to begin her life of full-time work

Sixteen-year-old **Laxmi**, Shantana's sister-in-law, works with her on the loom. Laxmi has been weaving for six years. She says:

> This work is good, because it gives us some income. But it is very bad, too... All day long we are sitting here, and it hurts our

backs and legs. Little pieces of wool come into our mouths and hurt our lungs, making us sick. Our fingers are raw and give us constant pain.[243]

The girls were advanced their weaving materials by a middleman, who charges them 1,000 rupees for the wool. When the carpet is finished they will sell it back to him; in the meantime, they earn no daily wages. After deductions for the cost of the materials, they are paid at the rate of sixty rupees per square foot of carpet. Between the two of them they can complete an average of half a square foot per day, for an effective daily wage of fifteen rupees. This is the fastest carpet knotting and the highest rate of earnings reported to Human Rights Watch by any of the carpet-making children—all of the others reported being able to knot about two inches a day, which translates into daily earnings of five to ten rupees.

With per-rug labor costs of 1,080 rupees and material costs of 1,000 rupees, the middleman's total cost for producing an eighteen foot carpet is 2,080 rupees, or about sixty dollars.

In addition to the advances of materials, the middlemen sometimes extend small loans of one hundred to one thousand rupees. This amount is then deducted from the payment for the rugs.

### Government Carpet Training Centers

The Indian government launched a training program for child carpet weavers in 1975, when India was anxious to increase its share of the global handwoven carpet market. Although the scheme was officially authorized to recruit children between the ages of twelve and fifteen, children six and up were brought into the program.[244] By 1981, 600 government carpet-weaving training centers were being run.[245] The program continues to this day, despite the passage of the 1986 Child Labour (Prohibition and Regulation) Act. The Child Labour (Prohibition and Regulation) Act strictly forbids the employment of children under fourteen in the carpet industry, due to its hazardous nature.

---

[243]  Ibid.

[244]  Anti-Slavery International, "Slavery Today in India," Factsheet B, July 1994.

[245]  Ibid. As of 1991, the number of government-run carpet-training centers was reported as approximately two hundred. Weiner, *The Child and the State in India*, p. 86.

Approximately sixty-five carpet training centers are in the state of Rajasthan.[246] Human Rights Watch visited one of these training centers, located in the town of Viratnagar. The center was a large single-roomed building in the center of town. About two dozen girls were seen to be working inside the dark and dimly lit building. The government  official in charge refused to let our investigators enter the building or speak to the girls, complaining about the negative influence of outsiders interfering with the government's role in employing carpet weavers. The girls appeared to be between ten and fourteen years old.

Trainees in these schools are paid a stipend of 250 rupees a month.[247] This has served as an inducement for many parents to withdraw their daughters from school and enroll them in the carpet centers. Although the training program ostensibly includes one hour daily of literacy instruction, this is rarely implemented.[248] An expert on child labor considers that:

> What is happening here is a repeat of the Bhadohi-Mirzapur [carpet belt] story. In the Bhadohi-Mirzapur area of Uttar Pradesh, a massive training programme for child weavers was introduced two decades ago as part of the Emergency-driven export promotion scheme. This naturally exacerbates the problem of child labour.[249]

### Applicable Law

The practices described above violate the Bonded Labour System (Abolition) Act and the Children (Pledging of Labour) Act. They also violate the Child Labour (Prohibition and Regulation) Act of 1986, which expressly forbids the employment of children in the carpet industry, which is deemed hazardous by

---

[246] Human Rights Watch interview with local children's rights activist, December 13, 1995, Viratnagar, Rajasthan.

[247] B. N. Juyal, "Official Schemes Exacerbate Situation in Northern States," *Vigil India*, No. 69, August 1995, p. 6.

[248] Ibid.

[249] Ibid. Under the Emergency of 1975-1977, then Prime Minister Indira Gandhi suspended civil liberties, arrested hundreds of opposition leaders and activists, and attempted to push through a number of economic reforms, including new development programs.

the act. The limited exceptions to this prohibition of child employment—exceptions for family-assisted production and production under the auspices of a government training program—themselves violate the Indian Constitution, which forbids the employment of any child under fourteen years of age in any hazardous employment.[250] Finally, the use of migrant bonded child laborers violates the Inter-State Migrant Workmen Act, and the Factories Act is violated in carpet units employing more than twenty people.

### Enforcement: the Carpet Belt

The carpet manufacturers and exporters are generally wealthy and powerful men, and legal action against them is extremely rare, especially when considered against the vast rate and number of abuses being committed by them.

As of 1992, not a single case of bonded labor had been prosecuted under the Bonded Labour System (Abolition) Act in Varanasi district, where both the carpet and silk industries rely heavily on bonded child labor.[251] About fifty cases had been brought against employers under the Child Labour (Prohibition and Regulation) Act, resulting in twenty-two convictions.[252] The maximum penalty imposed, however, was a fine of one hundred rupees, or about three dollars.[253] These low fines were levied notwithstanding the provisions of the act, which specify that first offenses are to be punished by three to twelve months in jail or a fine of 10,000 to 20,000 rupees.

When Human Rights Watch met with the Mirzapur district collector in December, 1995, he acknowledged that "some news reports do say there is child labor in the carpet industry," adding that "until a detailed survey is conducted, we cannot say they [the reports] are true."[254] Regarding bonded child labor, he said that when he heard rumors of it, he sent officials to investigate, but that so far they had found "very few" cases of bonded child labor. According to the district collector, at the time of our meeting he had seven or eight prosecutions pending for

---

[250] Indian Constitution, Article 24.

[251] Gargan, "Bound to Looms..."

[252] McDonald, "Boys of bondage ..." p. 19 .

[253] Ibid.

[254] Human Rights Watch interview with Mirzapur District Collector Bachittar Singh, December 19, 1995, Mirzapur, Uttar Pradesh.

violations of child labor laws. He was unable to provide figures for previous prosecutions, the rate of convictions, and fines levied. No one had been imprisoned in Mirzapur district for illegal labor practices.

One enforcement difficulty mentioned by the Mirzapur district collector and other state officials is the ineffectiveness of most workplace raids. According to these government officials, it is impossible to catch an employer breaking the law red-handed, because as soon as a stranger approaches all the children will run off. This has not hampered the work of the nongovernmental organizations Bonded Labour Liberation Front and South Asian Coalition Against Child Servitude, however. During the past decade, these groups have rescued thousands of children from servitude in the carpet and other industries. Occasionally, their liberation raids are accompanied by police officers. Their success indicates that it is in fact possible to act directly against the offending employers.

### Enforcement: Rajasthan

According to the Labour Commissioner for Rajasthan, Ashok Shekhar, the carpet industry is wrongly included in the Child Labour (Prohibition and Regulation) Act as a hazardous industry:

> We don't consider it hazardous. It was added to the list only because of pressure from the West. Children working in the carpet industry are in good health, they work in a good atmosphere... it is important that they be allowed to do this work... their nimble fingers make them well-suited for it, and it is good for them to learn as child apprentices.[255]

Commissioner Shekhar reported that he was in the process of submitting a petition to the government, on behalf of the Labour Commission of Rajasthan, requesting that carpet weaving be removed from the list of hazardous occupations.

Commissioner Shekhar readily admitted that Rajasthan has extensive numbers of children working in the carpet trade. As it is the Labour Commissioner who is responsible for enforcement of the Child Labour (Prohibition and Regulation) Act, however, it is not surprising that no carpet manufacturer or employer had been charged with violating the act in Rajasthan. In fact, the state did not even formulate its rules for enforcement of the act until September 1995, and that only after a local children's rights organization filed suit against the state.

---

[255] Human Rights Watch interview with Rajasthan Labour Commissioner Ashok Shekhar, December 15, 1995, Jaipur, Rajasthan.

In its petition, the organization described "callous indifference, nay, neglect, on the part of the various State functionaries responsible for protecting the interests of children in the State of Rajasthan."[256] As of July 1996, the state's Child Labour (Prohibition and Regulation) Act rules still had not been implemented.

Regarding bonded labor by children and adults, the Labour Commissioner for Rajasthan said, "Frankly, I don't think it exists in Rajasthan." He then said that there was "technical bonded labour" in the state, which he described as situations where an employer will give an advance of 10,000 or 20,000 rupees in order to secure a skilled worker, and then not let that employee leave until the advance is repaid. "But I would not say that is really bondage," he said. Commissioner Shekhar also alleged that social activists agitate around the issue of bonded labor where it does not exist in an attempt to extort mine owners and other employers.

Rajasthan was one of the states ordered by the Supreme Court in 1995 to report on the incidence of bonded labor within its jurisdiction. As in the other twelve states so ordered, the government of Rajasthan submitted an affidavit denying that bonded labor occurred there. The Supreme Court questioned the veracity of these reports and, on August 7, 1995, assigned thirteen teams of investigators, one for each state, to independently investigate the phenomenon of bonded labor in those states.[257] Each team was composed of an attorney and a social activist. In Rajasthan, Human Rights Watch spoke with the activist who reported on bonded labor to the court.[258] She had found that bondage was extensive in the state among both adults and children, including bondage of entire families as single units. The Rajasthani occupations where bondage is most rampant are agriculture, stone quarry work, and the brick kilns. Bondage among child domestic servants is also quite common.

---

[256] S. B. Civil Writ Petition No. 263/1995, *Ugam Raj Mohnot* v. *State of Rajasthan and Others*, filed January 18, 1995, before the High Court of Judicature for Rajasthan, Jaipur Bench, Jaipur. The writ requests, *inter alia*, that the Court "direct the State Government to make Rules under the Child Labour (Prohibition and Regulation) Act, 1986, and to implement the provisions of this act forthwith strictly..." The petitioner is coordinator of the Rajasthan branch of the Centre of Concern for Child Labour (CFCCL) and he filed the petition on behalf of the organization.

[257] Civ. Writ Petition No. 3922 of 1985 with Civ. Writ Petition No. 153 of 1982, Record of Proceedings, August 7, 1995.

[258] Human Rights Watch interview with Ms. Srilata Swaminathan, Rajasthan Kisan Sangathan, December 13, 1995, Jaipur, Rajasthan.

# VI. THE ROLE OF THE INDIAN GOVERNMENT

*It is not poverty which prevents India from investing more in its children, but rather the prejudices and values of those who create and implement policy in India.*[259]

When it comes to child labor, the Indian government has an impressive number of protective laws, government decrees and orders, national policies and projects, standing and special committees and commissions, and reports and recommendations.   Unfortunately, the laws are rarely enforced and the recommendations are rarely carried out.  Based on the facts—what is done rather than what is said—one must conclude that the Indian government is either unwilling to or uninterested in seriously tackling bonded child labor.

This chapter looks at how and why the Indian government says so much about child labor while doing so little to combat it.  It includes an overview of government programs and initiatives, efforts and omissions in implementing those initiatives, and the blatant failure of the government to protect its children by enforcing the law.

## GOVERNMENT POLICY, PROGRAMS, AND INITIATIVES

The Indian government has generally not addressed bonded child labor directly.  Instead, it has created and administered (to a limited extent) programs regarding child labor overall and bonded labor overall.  As a consequence, the unique vulnerability of the bonded child laborer, who falls at the intersection of these two groups, is ignored in nearly all government papers and plans for action.

### Government Programs Regarding Child Labor[260]

On August 15, 1994, India's Independence Day, then-Prime Minister P. V. Narasimha Rao announced his intention to bring two million child laborers out of hazardous industries by the year 2000.  One hundred and thirty-two districts spread across eleven states have been selected for the implementation of this

---

[259] Commission on Labour Standards and International Trade, *Child Labour in India...*, p. 41.

[260] This section discusses the government's child labor programs.  These are not programs designed specifically to address the needs of bonded child laborers; as of July 1996, the Indian government has no such program.

118

plan.[261] The districts were chosen because of their high incidence of child labor in industries defined as hazardous by the 1986 Child Labour (Prohibition and Regulation) Act, particularly the beedi, match, carpet, and glass industries. Widespread child bondage was not a factor in their selection, although as a practical matter both the beedi and carpet industries are heavily bonded. (While not typically marked by bondage, the conditions for both glass and match workers are brutal, with match-makers generally considered to be among the worst-off of India's child laborers.)

The Prime Minister's proposal, while only the latest in a long series of government proclamations and programs, was the first to set a specific target goal for the reduction of child labor.[262]  Two months after the Prime Minister's announcement, the Labour Ministry set up the National Authority for the Elimination of Child Labour.[263]  The Authority has three functions:

1. To lay down the policies and programmes for elimination of child labour particularly in hazardous employments.
2. To monitor the progress of implementation of [these programmes]...
3. To coordinate implementation of child labour elimination related projects of the various sister Ministries of the Government of India.[264]

The core of the Elimination of Child Labour Programme is the implementation of incentives designed to lure working children away from their jobs and into "special schools" that emphasize non-formal education and vocational training.[265]  The key component is a payment of one hundred rupees to the

---

[261] UNICEF, "Child Labour: UNICEF India Position," 1995, p. 4. There are 467 districts in all of India.

[262] See Commission on Labour Standards and International Trade, *Child Labour in India...*, p. 42-45 (describing eighteen policies, laws, committees, etc. established by central government since 1921).

[263] Ibid., p. 45.

[264] Ibid.

[265] "Non-formal education" is typically part-time instruction that emphasizes basic literacy and life skills. It is geared toward working children.

participating children's families. The children also receive one daily meal while in school.

The one hundred rupee incentive was first initiated by the 1987 National Child Labour Policy. This policy, funded by international donor agencies[266] and administered by local nongovernmental organizations, established the first special schools to provide non-formal education to working children. As of 1995, this program ministered to 7,000 children.[267] The new Elimination of Child Labour Programme represents an expansion of this program, rather than a reworking of its tenets.[268]

Funding for these programs is uncertain. The Indian government has said it will need eight and a half billion rupees from 1995 to 2000 in order to accomplish the goal of removing two million children from hazardous industries.[269] Despite this estimate, only 344 million rupees—about 4 percent of the five-year estimated cost—was allocated for child labor elimination programs in 1995-1996.[270] At this rate of expenditure, the projected costs will be achieved in about 24.7 years, or in 2020-2021, and not by 2000. In addition, since 1995 the Indian government has repeatedly threatened to begin rejecting foreign aid earmarked for

---

[266] The majority of the funds for this program were provided by the International Programme on the Elimination of Child Labour (IPEC), a program of the International Labour Organisation. IPEC focuses on "the worst abuses of child labour: hazardous work, forced labour, the employment of working children who are less than 12 or 13 years old, girls and street children." The NGO Group for the Convention on the Rights of the Child, 1993, "Eliminating the Exploitation of Child Labour: International, national and local action," May 1993, p. 8.

[267] Commission on Labour Standards, "Child Labour in India," p. 49 (source: Ministry of Labour). Additional IPEC programs serve nearly 55,000 children. Ministry of Labour, Government of India, "Children and Work," Workshop of District Collectors/District Heads on "Elimination of Child Labour in Hazardous Occupations," New Delhi, September 13-14, 1995, p. 11.

[268] Ministry of Labour, "Children and Work," p. 5.

[269] "Data on Child Labour yet to be Compiled," *The Hindu*, April 10, 1995, p. 13. The article uses the figure of 850 crore rupees; one crore is equal to ten million.

[270] Ministry of Labour, "Children and Work," p. 5.

child labour programs, including the heavily-funded ILO IPEC program.[271] (As of July 1996 these threats had not been implemented.) Both the low appropriations and the threat to refuse future outside aid indicate that the necessary fiscal commitment to the Prime Minister's program is lacking.[272]

In addition to funding problems, many Indian social welfare organizations and activists are troubled by the narrow scope of the program. Child laborers in India are estimated to number between sixty and 115 million. Viewed against these figures, the government's goal of releasing two million children appears rather insignificant. Even against the government's own figures of approximately twenty million child laborers—a number that is based on the 1981 census and regarded as inaccurate[273]—the program would address only 10 percent of the country's child laborers. Furthermore, there is no indication that measures will be taken to effectively prevent the replacement of the released children by other child laborers. Despite these shortcomings, the Indian government has continued to present this

---

[271] "India has told the International Labour Organisation it requires no external financial assistance for the various remedial measures it is taking [to eliminate children from the workforce in hazardous industries]." "Collectors Meeting on Child Labour," *The Statesman* (Calcutta edition), September 10, 1995; "Government today informed the Rajya Sabha that it had rejected the offer by some countries to help India check the problem of child labour, saying it preferred to depend on its own resources." "India rejects aid to tackle child labour," *The Statesman*, March 12, 1996; "India spurns aid to abolish child labour," *Times of India*, February 11, 1996.

[272] The issue of foreign aid also underscores the government's sensitivity to external critiques of child labor in India. According to one diplomat in New Delhi, "the Indian government is known to have discouraged suggestions, including one from the European Union, for financial assistance." The diplomat attributed this stance to a desire by the government "to avoid any meddling in its programme for abolition of child labour," pointing out that international funding brings with it accountability for the use of funds, something the Indian government may wish to avoid. "India spurns aid," *Times of India*, Feb. 11, 1996. Others believe that the government is positioning the issue of external aid as a bargaining chip in the ongoing debate over a linkage between trade and labor. Under this view, "[i]f the developed countries demand that the pace of compliance with international labour standards should be faster... India could then ask for a substantial part of the cost of the programmes to be shared by the developed countries." Ibid.

[273] The twenty million figure was used by then-Prime Minister Rao on August 15, 1994, when he announced the government's goal of releasing two million child workers from hazardous industries by the year 2000. Campaign Against Child Labour, "Reference Kit for Media Persons," January 1995, p. 8.

program as its bold new answer to the problem of child labor, while remaining quiet about the fate of dozens of millions of child laborers outside its scope.

As pointed out by a joint government-nongovernmental organization report, effective action depends on an accurate assessment of the problem:

> The sense of urgency, the financial implication, and above all the manner in which the strategy to deal with child labour has to be phased, all depend on assessment of the magnitude of the problem. A wrong assessment, therefore, would lead to the formulation of a strategy which is unlikely to prove effective.[274]

The Indian government has been negligent in its refusal to collect and analyze current and relevant data regarding the incidence of child labor. As of 1996, official figures continue to be based on 1981 census figures, which counted thirteen and a half million working children below the age of fourteen. There is no internal consistency in the treatment of these figures by government officials; some cite figures extrapolated from the 1981 census—usually between seventeen and twenty million—while others continue to rely on the thirteen million figure.[275] Regardless of which of these figures are used, they are nowhere near the number estimated by leading national and international social scientists. UNICEF, for example, cites figures ranging from seventy-five to ninety million child laborers under the age of fourteen. [276] The census data for 1991 had not yet been compiled at the time of this writing.[277]

---

[274] Department of Women and Child Development, Indian Council for Child Welfare, and UNICEF, India Country Office, "Rights of the Child: Report of a National Consultation, November 21-23, 1994, p. 102.

[275] N.K. Doval, "Double-speak on child labour," *The Hindu*, December 28, 1994; Ministry of Labour, *Children and Work*, September 13-14, 1995. Based on 1981 figures, the Planning Commission for the Census of India estimated that there were seventeen and a half million child laborers under the age of fourteen in 1985, eighteen million in 1990, and 20 million in 1995 See Commission on Labour Standards, *Child Labour in India*, p. 3

[276] Gerry Pinto, UNICEF, "Child Labour in India: The Issue and Directions for Action," 1995, p. 2; UNICEF et al., "Rights of the Child," p. 101.

[277] Ministry of Labour, *Children and Work*, September 13-14, 1995, p. 2. Preliminary numbers released from the 1991 census include a total population of 844 million people, 298 million of whom are children under the age of fifteen. Of these children, 221

The cavalier treatment of child labor statistics underscores the Indian government's low prioritization of this issue. Other evidence of the government's lack of concern is its ineffectiveness in implementing the Elimination of Child Labor Programme. The crux of the program is the monthly one hundred rupee stipend, intended to make school a more attractive and realistic option to the working child. The money for the stipend is provided by the government—principally the Ministry of Labour[278]—and distributed by the local nongovernmental organizations who run the special schools.

In the course of our investigation, however, three different organizations in three different districts, representing among them dozens of special schools, told Human Rights Watch that the requisite governmental funds for this program had not been received in six to ten months. During this period, the students had not received their promised stipends, the daily meals had been reduced drastically in terms of both quality and quantity, and the teachers at the special schools had gone unpaid.

The administering organizations were extremely concerned by the government's failure to deliver these monies. They reported that the loss of the stipend had forced many children to drop out of school and return to the labor force. In the meantime, most who had not yet dropped out were being pressured to do so, either by family members or by former bondmasters/employers who the children were still in the process of paying off, with help from the government stipend.

The following story is a typical example of the deleterious effect of the loss of the one hundred rupee monthly stipend.

As reported in the chapter on carpets, Shivalinga, a thirteen-year-old, stopped working in 1994 with the support of a regional children's rights group. He had begun working in the carpet industry at the age of nine, when his father, a landless agricultural laborer, took a 2,000 rupee advance against his son. Shivalinga was paid just twenty-five to fifty rupees upon the completion of each rug—the equivalent of about one rupee per day. Had Shivalinga been paid at the rate of just ten rupees a day (which is far below minimum wage and would itself

---

million live in rural areas and seventy-one million in urban areas. These numbers are already considered out of date, with most sources reporting an overall population of more than 900 million. India's population is expected to cross the one billion mark by the turn of the century.

[278] Human Rights Watch interview with National Human Rights Commission, Secretary General R. V. Pillai, New Delhi, December 28, 1995.

constitute proof of a bonded labor relationship), he could have paid off the original loan in eight months and, in the remaining two-plus years of his employment, earned another 7,000 rupees. As it is, however, Shivalinga's former employer claims he is still owed the 2,000 rupee advance. The employer constantly harasses Shivalinga's father, telling him to either pay back the money or remove Shivalinga from school and send him back to the loom. Shivalinga's father intends to use the one hundred rupee stipend Shivalinga receives for going to the special school in order to pay back the owner. However, at the time Human Rights Watch interviewed Shivalinga, he had not received the stipend for ten months, with the result that his father was unable to make payments to the former employer. Shivalinga told Human Rights Watch that he was worried that he would be pulled out of school and returned to the looms. This had already happened to a friend of his.

### Government Programs Regarding Bonded Labor

News articles on bonded labor appear with regularity in Indian newspapers, always lamenting the continuing scourge of this age-old practice, a practice that at any given time is enslaving dozens of millions of Indian adults and children. Nonetheless, and in contrast to the frequent lip service paid to child labor problems, the Indian government has over the years stayed largely quiet on the topic of debt bondage.

Bonded labor was not abolished by law until 1975, when a government ordinance called for its immediate eradication. The following year, the Indian parliament passed the Bonded Labour System (Abolition) Act, the provisions of which continue to comprise the central government's sole "policy" and "program" regarding the practice of debt bondage.[279]

Enforcement of the act is the responsibility of state governments. The state governments in turn are expected to delegate all enforcement duties—including not only the release of bonded laborers but their rehabilitation as well—to the various district magistrates (also known as district collectors) of

---

[279] This chapter discusses only certain aspects of the Bonded Labour System (Abolition) Act. For a more comprehensive overview, see the chapters on the legal context of bonded child labor and on the beedi industry. The full text of the act may be found in the appendix.

their particular state.[280] The district magistrates are directed by the act to form "vigilance committees" regarding the eradication of bonded labor. These committees are intended to form the backbone of act enforcement.[281]

Notwithstanding this delegation of duties, the central government remains ultimately responsible for the effective implementation of the Bonded Labour System (Abolition) Act, and has considerable powers, both budgetary and rule-making, in directing the act's implementation by the states.

The central government's authority and responsibility for application of the act was acknowledged by the Indian Supreme Court in one of the first cases brought before it under the act. The court in this case "direct[ed] the Union of India to take up the matter [of act enforcement] with the State Governments and ensure that the vigilance committees have been constituted... as required by the act.[282]

When a person is identified as a bonded laborer by the government, she or he becomes immediately eligible not only for release from bondage but for rehabilitation as well. The right to rehabilitation originates in the Bonded Labour System (Abolition) Act, Art. 14(b) of which directs the vigilance committees "to provide for the economic and social rehabilitation of the freed-bonded labourers." This right to rehabilitation has been fleshed-out and solidified in subsequent formulations of act-related rules, in bonded-labor scheme updates worked out jointly by the central and state governments' Ministries of Labour, and in court cases.

According to the Supreme Court, the state's duty to identify, release, and "suitably rehabilitate" its bonded laborers is not only mandated by the Bonded Labour System (Abolition) Act, but is also required by the Indian Constitution.

> It is the plainest requirement of Articles 21 and 23 of the Constitution that bonded labourers must be identified and

---

[280] Bonded Labour (System Abolition) Act, Ch. IV, Art. 10, Art. 12 and Ch. V, Art. 14. There are twenty-five states in India and 467 districts. Stanley Wolpert, *India* (Berkeley: University of California Press, 1991), p. 199; UNICEF, "Child Labour: UNICEF India Position," 1995, p. 4.

[281] See chapter on applicable law for details of the committees' duties.

[282] Judgement in Writ Petition No. 1187, 1982 (cited in Vivek Pandit, "Prevention of Atrocities (Scheduled Castes/Scheduled Tribes): Bonded Labour, Their Rights and Implementation", 1995), p. 7.

released and on release, they must be suitably rehabilitated....
[A]ny failure of action on the part of the State Government[s] in
implementing the provisions of [the Bonded Labour System
(Abolition) Act] would be the clearest violation of Article 21
[and] Article 23 of the Constitution."[283]

Article 21 of the Indian Constitution guarantees the right to life and liberty; Article
23 prohibits the practice of debt bondage and other forms of forced labor or
slavery.[284]

The court's conclusion that rehabilitation is a constitutional requirement
recognizes the fact that, without rapid and effective rehabilitation efforts, freed
bonded laborers will quickly relapse into bondage once more. A bonded laborer
is by definition a person without resources, without land, and without options of
any sort, including, for reasons largely related to caste, the possibility of
occupational mobility. Freeing a bonded laborer without working to alter the
underlying foundation of his or her bondage is a half measure. As the Supreme
Court said:

> [I]t would be nothing short of cruelty and heartlessness to
> identify and release bonded labourers merely to throw them at
> the mercy of the existing social and economic system which
> denies them even the basic necessities of life... What use are
> "identification" and "release" to bonded labourers if after
> attaining their so-called freedom from bondage to a master they
> are consigned to a life of another bondage, namely, bondage to
> hunger and starvation where they have nothing to hope for, not
> even anything to die for... What would they prize more:
> freedom and liberty with hunger and destitution staring them in
> the face or some food to satisfy their hunger and the hunger of
> their near and dear ones, even at the cost of freedom and liberty?
> The answer is obvious. It is therefore imperative that neither the
> Government nor the Court should be content with merely
> securing identification and release of bonded labourers but every
> effort must be made by them to see that the freed bonded

---

[283] *Neeraja Chaudhary* v. *State of Madhya Pradesh*, 3 SCC, paragraphs 243, 255
(1984).

[284] For details, see chapter on applicable law.

labourers are properly and suitably rehabilitated after identification and release.[285]

Another writer, a human rights lawyer with extensive experience working with bonded laborers, put it more bluntly. "A bonded labourer who becomes free without the means to survive," he wrote, "becomes free to die."[286]

As of 1996, a bonded laborer identified and released by the state is entitled to a rehabilitation allowance of 6,250 rupees. The 1994-1995 annual report of the Indian government's Ministry of Labour reported that in August 1994, state and central government labor officials agreed to raise the rehabilitation allowance to 10,000 rupees.[287] Nonetheless, as of July 1996, this raise had not been effectuated.

The failure of state governments to comply with their legal obligations under the Bonded Labour System (Abolition) Act—particularly the formation and adequate functioning of the district-level vigilance committees—is one of the primary reasons behind the low enforcement rate of the law and the continuing high prevalence of bonded labor. (Indeed, by some accounts, bonded labor is actually increasing during the 1990s.[288]) Another contributing factor, mentioned previously in the context of child labor policy, is the failure of the government to gather and maintain accurate or even plausible statistics.

The statistics problem is as acute in the bonded labor context as it is in the child labor context. According to credible estimates, the number of bonded laborers in India is approximately sixty-five million, representing slightly more than 7 percent of the country's total population.[289] Certain individual states alone are estimated to have bonded labor populations of one to two million people; a report from Tamil Nadu, based on extensive research conducted at the direction of

---

[285] *Neeraja Chaudhary* v. *State of Madhya Pradesh*, 3 SCC 243, paragraphs 245-246 (1984).

[286] Pandit, "Bonded Labour," p. 18.

[287] Ministry of Labour, *Annual Report 1994-1995*, p. 97.

[288] See, e.g., Mahajan and Gathia, *Child Labour: An Analytical Study*, p. 25. Not only is the incidence of bonded child labor increasing, but the wages paid to bonded laborers are steadily decreasing in real terms. S.P. Tiwary, "Bondage in Santhal Parganas," *Chains of Servitude...*, p. 206.

[289] "Citizen's [sic] Body on Bonded Labour," *Times of India*, November 18, 1994.

the Supreme Court, concluded that there were "well over 10 lakhs" (one million) bonded laborers working in that state.[290] Other states known to have high rates of bondage include Andhra Pradesh, Karnataka, Madhya Pradesh, Maharashtra, Gujarat, Rajasthan, Uttar Pradesh, Haryana, and Bihar.

In contrast to the figures used by social scientists, the Indian government's figures regarding bonded labor are unconvincingly low. The central Ministry of Labour relies on the state Ministries of Labour—which are charged with enforcing the Bonded Labour System (Abolition) Act—to report the number of bonded laborers identified, released, and rehabilitated. Based on information submitted by the states, the central Ministry of Labour's 1994-1995 Annual Report stated that the nationwide target for 1994-1995 was the rehabilitation of 2,784 bonded laborers—a figure representing less than .005 percent of all estimated bonded laborers. The figure for the total number of bonded laborers identified, when viewed in contrast to the same figures provided in 1989, illustrate the lack of implementation of the Bonded Labour (Abolition) Act. In 1989, the total number of bonded laborers identified was 242,532.[291] By 1995, this number had risen to 251,424.[292] These figures indicate that from 1988 to 1995, only 8,892 bonded laborers had been identified throughout the country, at a time when nongovernmental sources were reporting that there were as many as sixty-five million bonded laborers in India by 1994.[293] Ironically, in the paragraph following the presentation of statistics in the 1994-95 *Annual Report*, the report states that "[t]he [state] Governments are attaching the highest priority to the total eradication of the bonded labour system in the country."[294]

The central government's reliance on and acceptance of state government statistics regarding bonded labor is misplaced and irresponsible. The majority of

---

[290] *Report of the Commission on Bonded Labour in Tamilnadu*, October 31, 1995, Madras, p. 208, Part VIII, para. A. This report was submitted by order of the Supreme Court in connection with Supreme Court Civ. Writ Petition No. 3922 of 1985 (*Public Union for Civil Liberties* v. *State of Tamil Nadu and Others*).

[291] Sarma, *Welfare of Special Categories of Labour*, p. 55, citing 1989-90 Ministry of Labour statistics.

[292] Ministry of Labour, *Annual Report 1994-95*, p. 97.

[293] "Citizen's [sic] Body on Bonded Labour," *Times of India*, November 18, 1994.

[294] Ibid.

state governments vastly underreport the incidence of bonded labor within their borders. For instance, the government of Tamil Nadu, where an independent commission recently concluded that there existed more than one million bonded laborers, stated in a sworn affidavit to the Supreme Court that "in Tamil Nadu, only stray cases of bonded labour are noticed..."[295] Twelve other state governments made the same assertion to the court, which expressed its disbelief by ordering independent investigations into the matter.[296]

In interviews with Human Rights Watch, top labor officials from the states of Gujarat and Rajasthan, both states with high levels of debt bondage, asserted that there was no bonded labor in their states. "I frankly don't think it [bonded labor] exists in Rajasthan," said Ashok Shekhar, Labour Commissioner for Rajasthan; one of his subordinates added that, "there is no case of bonded labour in Rajasthan."[297] When asked about the reports of widespread bondage from journalists and activists, Commissioner Shekhar conceded, as noted, that there might exist "technical bonded labour," whereby an advance is paid to secure a worker's labor, but he insisted that this practice was "not really bondage." He also said that activists who organize against bonded labor practices in the stone quarries of Rajasthan are not acting on behalf of the bonded laborers, but rather are hoping to be paid off by the owners in order to stay quiet. Ashok Bhasin, the Deputy Labour Commissioner for the neighboring state of Gujarat, concurred with

---

[295] Affidavit on behalf of the State Government of Tamil Nadu, October 7, 1994. This affidavit was submitted by order of the Supreme Court in connection with Supreme Court Civ. Writ Petition No. 3922 of 1985 (*Public Union for Civil Liberties* v. *State of Tamil Nadu and Others*).

[296] The case that sparked this inquiry, *Public Union for Civil Liberties* v. *State of Tamil Nadu and Others*, was filed in 1985. Much of the delay in its resolution is due to the state governments' failure to respond to court directives in a timely manner. In its order requiring the states to report on bonded labor practices, the court noted that "It does appear to us that no significant progress has been made by the concerned authorities and it is not unlikely that the attitude of the concerned authorities is not enthusiastic as one would expect in a matter of such significance." Record of Proceedings, May 13, 1994. As of August 1996, Human Rights Watch has been unable to find out whether the case has been resolved.

[297] Human Rights Watch interview with Ashok Shekhar, Labour Commissioner for Rajasthan, December 15, 1995, Jaipur, Rajasthan.

Commissioner Shekhar's statements. As for his own state, he asserted that "bonded labour does not exist in Gujarat... neither among women, men, or children."[298]

Dr. Manoj Dayal, a professor at the University of Allahabad described how the government of Bihar "abolished" bonded labor:

> As soon as the issue of abolishing bonded labour was raised in Bihar, the State Government outrightly persisted that there was no system of bonded labour prevailing in the State; that what exists in the State is a system of attached labour and that the labourers are assured of remuneration, cultivable and homestead land, clothing, interest-free loans and so on. The Bihar Government thus abolished bonded labour by redefining it and by terming it as "attached labour system."[299]

Given this willful denial of one of the country's most pressing social ills, it is not surprising that government officials' efforts on behalf of bonded laborers have remained meager at best. The failure to address the issue is doubly egregious in the case of bonded child laborers, who, without intervention, will be doomed to pass their entire lives in a state of virtual slavery.

## FAILURE OF THE INDIAN GOVERNMENT TO ENFORCE THE LAW

*An analysis of data indicating the number of prosecutions launched under [the Child Labour] Act and convictions obtained would clearly indicate that this act ... has achieved very little.*[300]

The government's failure to enforce the Child Labour (Prohibition and Regulation) Act and the government's failure to enforce the Bonded Labour System (Abolition) Act—not to mention the failure to enforce the several other laws protecting child workers—are twin manifestations of the same set of

---

[298]    Human Rights Watch interview with Ashok Bhasin, Deputy Labour Commissioner for Gujarat, December 15, 1995, Jaipur, Rajasthan.

[299]  Manoj Dayal, "Abolition of Bonded Labour an Eye-wash in Bihar," *Patrika*, December 26, 1995.

[300]  Department of Women and Child Development, Indian Council for Child Welfare, UNICEF-India, "Rights of the Child: Report of a National Consultation, November 21-23, 1994, p. 102.

phenomena. These phenomena include apathy, caste and class bias, obstruction of enforcement efforts, corruption, low prioritization of the problem, and disregard for the deep and widespread suffering of bonded child laborers.

### Enforcement Statistics

A glaring sign of neglect of their duties by officials charged with enforcing child labor laws is the failure to collect, maintain, and disseminate accurate statistics regarding enforcement efforts. Human Rights Watch met with a top official of the Ministry of Labour, but he was unable to provide any statistics regarding enforcement of the Child Labour (Prohibition and Regulation) Act or other legislation protecting the rights of child workers.[301] We attempted to meet with S. S. Sharma, the Director General of Labour Welfare and, as such, the official entrusted with enforcement of the Bonded Labour System (Abolition) Act. Director-General Sharma refused to grant an interview to Human Rights Watch while we were in New Delhi, suggesting instead that we fax him a set of questions, which we did. Unfortunately, we received no response.[302] The enforcement statistics that follow have been gleaned from a variety of sources, including public government documents, news reports, and interviews with government officials.

### Child Labour (Prohibition and Regulation) Act

At the national level, from 1990 to 1993, 537 inspections were carried out under the Child Labour (Prohibition and Regulation) Act. These inspections turned

---

[301] The inability to come up with basic statistics regarding enforcement was not an aberration, but rather just one example of a chronic failure to keep—and make public—this information. See, e.g., "Scheme to divert kids from hazardous units," *Indian Express,* February 27, 1995.

[302] The questions we asked of the Director General of Labour Welfare included questions regarding: agency estimates of the number of bonded child laborers in India; the number of district vigilance committees currently in operation, and their activities to date; the number of cases prosecuted under the Bonded Labour System (Abolition) Act and the results of these prosecutions; the number of people rehabilitated under the Bonded Labour System (Abolition) Act; whether any bonded child laborers have ever been rehabilitated under the act; and the agency opinion regarding the case of bonded labor currently before the Supreme Court, in which thirteen states are accused of allowing widespread bonded labor to flourish.

up 1,203 violations. Inexplicably, only seven prosecutions were launched.[303] At the state level, the years 1990 to 1993 produced 60,717 inspections in which 5,060 violations of the act were detected; 772 of these 5,060 violations resulted in convictions.[304]

At the state level during the 1993 to 1994 year, the latest period for which data are available, 1,596 cases were filed against employers.[305] The number of convictions is unknown; many of these cases may still be pending.

When convictions are obtained under the Child Labour (Prohibition and Regulation) Act, the fines are light. The vast majority of adjudicated offenders receive fines of five dollars or less—just a few hundred rupees, as opposed to the 10,000 to 20,000 fine stipulated by the act itself.[306] To the knowledge of Human Rights Watch, not a single case brought under the act has resulted in imprisonment, to date, although the act allows for sentences of three months to a year for first-time offenders and six months to two years for repeat offenders.[307]

Some information is available from various states of India regarding enforcement of the Child Labour (Prohibition and Regulation) Act. In Tamil Nadu, the act was not enforced until 1994—eight years after its passage—when a case

---

[303] Commission on Labour Standards and International Trade, *Child Labour in India: A Perspective*, June 10, 1995, p. 33. Inspections by the national government presumable took place in New Delhi and other centrally-administered territories.

[304] Ibid.

[305] N.K. Doval,"Double-Speak on Child Labour," *The Hindu*, December 28, 1994.

[306] Molly Moore, "Poverty Weaves Harshness Into Lives," *Guardian Weekly*, June 4, 1995, p. 19 (reprint from *Washington Post*) (of 4,000 convictions reported under the Act since 1986, 3,500 offenders got off with a fine equivalent to five dollars or less; figures from report by an Indian Chamber of Commerce and the International Labour Organisation). The assertion that there have been 4,000 convictions under the act does not coincide with the data released by the government regarding 1990 to 1993 convictions, reported above. The government's figures of 772 convictions for one three year period indicate that, since the act was passed in 1986, total convictions probably number 2,500 or less.

[307] Hema Shukla, "India Insincere in Ending Child Labor," United Press International, September 12, 1994.

was filed in North Arcot district.[308] In the two years since then, according to a senior state official, there have been fifteen or sixteen convictions under the Child Labour (Prohibition and Regulation) Act, and another fifty cases or so are pending.[309] To date, no one has been imprisoned in Tamil Nadu for violation of either the Child Labour (Prohibition and Regulation) Act or the Bonded Labour System (Abolition) Act. According to activists in the state, on the rare occasions when prosecutions of Child Labour (Prohibition and Regulation) Act offenders are mounted by the state, some judicial magistrates are quick to dismiss the charges, ostensibly for lack of evidence, but in fact because of corruption or sympathy with the defendant employers.[310]

In the Firozabad district of Uttar Pradesh, more than 50,000 children are estimated to be working in glass factories in violation of the Factories Act and the Child Labour (Prohibition and Regulation) Act.[311] Nonetheless, in 1995 there were only two convictions for child labor law violations in Firozabad, and the assistant labour commissioner, Mr. B. K. Singh, told a journalist that "[t]here is no child labour in the district now."[312] According to the Secretary General of the National Human Rights Commission, the enforcement problem, in Firozabad and elsewhere, is "just a matter of people not doing their work."[313]

---

[308] Human Rights Watch interview with North Arcot District Collector M. P. Vijaykumar, November 27, 1995, Vellore, Tamil Nadu.

[309] Human Rights Watch interview with senior state official, a former district collector of Tamil Nadu, November 22, 1995, Madras, Tamil Nadu.

[310] Human Rights Watch interviews, November 17 - December 1, 1995, Tamil Nadu.

[311] Human Rights Watch interview with social activists, December 22, 1995, Firozabad, Uttar Pradesh. See also Burra, *Born to Work*, p. xxiii (of 200,000 glass workers in Firozabad, 50,000 are children).

[312] Srawan Shukla, "Childhood goes up in Smoke in the 'Land of Glass,'" *Times of India*, November 19, 1994.

[313] Human Rights Watch interview with R. V. Pillai, Secretary General, National Human Rights Commission, December 28, 1995, New Delhi.

### Bonded Labour System (Abolition) Act

Official statistics reflecting enforcement of the Bonded Labour System (Abolition) Act are equally difficult to obtain. Statistics regarding application of the Bonded Labour System (Abolition) Act to children are nonexistent. Indeed, at least some government officials interviewed by Human Rights Watch appeared to be laboring under the conviction that the Bonded Labour System (Abolition) Act does not apply to children, an interpretation that has no basis in the law itself nor in Supreme Court cases interpreting the law.

As of March 1993, the latest date for which official figures are available, state governments had reported the identification and release of a total of 251,424 bonded laborers. This number indicates all bonded laborers identified and released since the Bonded Labour System (Abolition) Act was passed in 1976.[314] Of this number, 227,404 were reported to have been rehabilitated.[315] If this number includes any rehabilitated bonded child laborers, that fact has not been reported.

State governments' statistics grossly under-report the current incidence of bonded labor. As mentioned, the Supreme Court has been examining the incidence of bonded labor in thirteen states.[316] These thirteen states, chosen by the court for investigation because of their reputation for high rates of debt bondage, all claimed in affidavits to the court that there was little or no bonded labor within their jurisdictions.[317] The court, skeptical of these claims, appointed teams of investigators to study the issue in each state.[318]

When districts and states do report on statistics regarding the identification and rehabilitation of bonded laborers, these numbers are frequently unreliable. The team investigating bonded labor in Tamil Nadu, for example, found that

---

[314] Ministry of Labour, *Annual Report 1994-1995*, pp. 96-97.

[315] Ibid., p. 97.

[316] The case, *Public Union for Civil Liberties* v. *State of Tamil Nadu and Others* (Civ. Writ Petition No. 3922 of 1985), is investigating the practice of bonded labor, and the states' failure to eradicate that practice, in the states of Karnataka, Madhya Pradesh, Kerala, Andhra Pradesh, Rajasthan, Haryana, West Bengal, Bihar, Uttar Pradesh, Maharashtra, Tamil Nadu, Gujarat, and Meghalaya.

[317] *Public Union for Civil Liberties* v. *State of Tamil Nadu and Others*, Civ. Writ Petition No. 3922 of 1985 with Civ. Writ Petition No. 153 of 1982, Record of Proceedings, August 7, 1995, p. 2.

[318] Ibid., p. 3.

"[s]tatutory registers relating to bonded labour were not maintained in many districts."[319] Simple neglect or lack of resources is not the only or even the primary reason for lack of accurate statistics. According to the investigative team, "Details provided by the state government and the district administration do not tally in most districts and even appear fabricated."[320]

This can be seen in states' statistics on bonded labor which are submitted to the central government. For example, there are at least three examples from 1988 to 1995 where states have reported that the number of bonded laborers that have been rehabilitated are greater than the number of bonded laborers that have been identified. In 1988, the state of Tamil Nadu reported that 34,640 bonded laborers had been rehabilitated, but they also reported that 33,581 bonded laborers had been identified, meaning that the state claimed it had rehabilitated 1,059 more people than it had ever identified as bonded laborers.[321] In the 1989-90 report to the Ministry of Labour, the state of Orissa reported that 51,751 bonded laborers had been rehabilitated, but only 48,657 had been identified.[322] The state of Tamil Nadu reported in the 1994-95 Ministry of Labour Annual Report that 39,054 bonded laborers had been rehabilitated, but they had identified 38,886.[323] In total, these three examples indicate that 4,321 more people were rehabilitated than were identified as bonded laborers.

These statistics are disturbing for two reasons. The first is that these statistics are cumulative totals, meaning that every year, new cases are added to the cases from previous years, dating back to 1976, when the Bonded Labour System (Abolition) Act became law, so that the yearly statistics represent the total number of bonded laborers that have ever been identified, released, and rehabilitated. The second factor that makes the statistics suspect is that before bonded laborers can be eligible for rehabilitation, they must be identified as bonded laborers. Because of

---

[319] G. V. Krishnan,"TN has 10 Lakh [one million] Bonded Workers, says Panel," *Times of India*, March 1, 1996.

[320] Ibid.

[321] Reddy, *Bonded Labour System in India*, p. 153. Citing 1988-89 Ministry of Labour statistics.

[322] Sarma, *Welfare of Special Categories of Labour*, p. 55, citing 1989-90 Ministry of Labour statistics.

[323] Ministry of Labour, *Annual Report 1994-95*, p.97.

this methodology, the cumulative totals for rehabilitation can never be more than the cumulative totals for identification and when this occurs, such as the previous three cases, it indicates a serious flaw in reporting. This may be due to several factors: state governments may be arbitrarily determining bonded labor statistics, or the inaccuracies may be due to simple error, or people who were not bonded laborers are being rehabilitated as bonded laborers. In one example of the latter, a survey of 180 bonded laborers who had been officially rehabilitated by the Bihar government found that 120 had never been bonded.[324]

Another indication that the law is not being enforced is the fact much of the money allocated for the rehabilitation of bonded laborers is unspent and reabsorbed by the government. Funding for rehabilitation is allocated through a fifty-fifty matching grant in which the states undertake rehabilitation and the central government matches their expenditures.[325] It is administered through several schemes under the Integrated Rural Development Program (IRDP) and Jawahar Rozgar Yojana (JRY). Records of expenditures for these programs show that in 1989-90, only 76.16 percent of the funds were utilized. In 1990-91, 78.41 percent of funds were utilized. And in 1991-92, only 47.83 percent of funds available were utilized for rehabilitating bonded laborers.[326] On March 14, 1996, the Parliamentary Committee on Labour and Welfare reported that only 38.39 percent of the funds available for the rehabilitation of bonded laborers had been utilized. The reason given was that "the state governments failed to submit certificates in regard to the expenditure incurred by them. Because of this lapse, the Central government did not release funds to them."[327] The failure to report expenditures indicates a failure to enforce the law.

A Supreme Court lawyer closely connected to bonded labor litigation corroborated the unreliable nature of the district collectors' reports, saying there is "no mechanism to ascertain [the collectors'] veracity."[328] According to this

---

[324] Manoj Dayal, "Abolition of Bonded Labour an Eye-wash in Bihar," *Patrika*, December 26, 1995.

[325] Ministry of Labour, *Annual Report 1994-95*, p. 97.

[326] Hoshiar Singh, *Administration of Rural Development in India* (New Delhi: Sterling Publishers Pvt. Ltd., 1995), pp.165-188.

[327] "Allocations for Labour Schemes Unutilised," *Times of India*, March 15, 1996.

[328] Human Rights Watch interview, December 29, 1995, New Delhi.

advocate and others familiar with the issue, corruption in application of the Bonded Labour System (Abolition) Act and dispersal of act-related rehabilitation funds is common. "A collector may receive 100,000 rupees for rehabilitation efforts but disperse only 10,000 of it. Embezzlement is difficult to track, but we all know it happens. For example, a bonded labourer comes in, puts his thumb print on the document saying he will receive 6,250 rupees, but receives only 3,000 rupees."[329]

Corruption and neglect are not the only reasons for bad statistics regarding bonded labor. Another is passivity on the part of enforcing officials, who too often take no affirmative steps to discover and root out debt bondage in their districts. Whether this is due to simple apathy or to a misunderstanding on their part of their official duties, the effect is disastrous for bonded laborers, who are left in their state of enslavement indefinitely. In Tamil Nadu, for example, the investigators found that "most District Collectors... had one basis to assume that bonded labour does not exist—No one is coming forward [to report that they are in bondage]."[330]

Human Rights Watch was unable to obtain any statistics on prosecution under the Bonded Labour System (Abolition) Act after 1988.[331] Up to 1988, there were 7,000 prosecutions under the Bonded Labour (Abolition) Act throughout India, of which 700 resulted in convictions.[332] It is certain that prosecution under the act is rare. In Tamil Nadu, the first prosecutions under the twenty-year-old act occurred in 1995, when eight beedi employers were arrested by the North Arcot District Collector.[333] The case, which drew headlines in the regional press, was depicted as a bold "get tough" measure. The agents spent one night in jail and

---

[329] Ibid. See also Reddy, *Bonded Labour System in India*, p. 171.

[330] Report of the Commission on Bonded Labour in Tamil Nadu, October 31, 1995, Madras, submitted for Supreme Court Civ. Writ Petition No. 3922 of 1985, Part V, p. 1.

[331] We asked the Director General of Labour Welfare for India for these statistics, but he declined to respond.

[332] Reddy, *Bonded Labour System in India*, p.161.

[333] Human Rights Watch interview with District Collector M. P. Vijaykumar, November 27, 1995, Vellore, Tamil Nadu.

were fined 500 rupees each.[334] The Bonded Labour System (Abolition) Act allows
for punishment of three years in prison and a 2,000 rupee fine.

### Obstacles to Enforcement

#### Apathy
The endemic apathy among government officials charged with enforcing
India's labor laws is apparent at all levels: national, state, and district. While
undoubtedly there are many committed men and women among their
ranks—including, for example, the district collector of North Arcot in Tamil Nadu,
whom Human Rights Watch interviewed—such commitment is not the norm.
From India's top labor officials all the way down to the local level, where tehsildars
(community leaders) use their influence to support the status quo, Human Rights
Watch and other researchers have found a profound lack of concern for the plight
of bonded and child laborers.

There are many concrete examples of government neglect. The Child
Labour (Prohibition and Regulation) Act, signed into law in 1986, requires each
state to formulate rules for its implementation. Until this is done, the law cannot
be applied in those states. As of July 1996, a full ten years after the act's birth, the
majority of states have failed to formulate and implement these necessary rules.[335]
It is a sign of the government's disregard of this issue that we are unable to report
the exact number of India's twenty-five states that have made rules for the act's
application. When we asked a very senior official of the central Ministry of
Labour—who spoke only on condition of anonymity—how many states had made
rules under the Child Labour (Prohibition and Regulation) Act, he said "I don't
know." He then said, "Laws don't matter. Economics do," and went on to assert
that, until rural prosperity increases, nothing can be done about child labor.

---

[334] Ibid. See also "8 Beedi Agents held under Bonded Labour System (Abolition)
Act," *Indian Express*, September 10, 1995.

[335] Commission on Labour Standards and International Trade, *Child Labour in
India...*, p. 9 ("There is also apathy amongst State Governments. Most states do not have
yet in place the framing of rules for the enforcement of the Child Labour (Prohibition and
Regulation) Act of 1986, nearly a decade later!"). The Commission on Labour Standards
and International Trade was appointed by the Indian government in August 1994 for the
purpose of studying "Issues Concerning the Protection of Labour Rights and Related
Matters." Ibid., appendix 1.

Clearly, states are receiving no pressure from the national government to implement the Child Labour (Prohibition and Regulation) Act. Nor, for the most part, are they themselves taking the initiative to push for greater enforcement of child labor legislation. It is at the district level that most enforcement efforts are coordinated and carried out, and these efforts are managed and overseen by the district magistrates. The district magistrates, or collectors as they are also called, are civil servants appointed by the state ministers, and are the top law enforcement and administrative authorities at the district level. At a 1995 conference of district magistrates and collectors in New Delhi, various district heads told a journalist that child labor was "very low" on their list of priorities, ranking about twenty-fifth (investment in high-tech industries was first).[336]

Regarding the Bonded Labour System (Abolition) Act, the government's egregious neglect of the law is most evident in the nearly universal failure of districts to form the requisite vigilance committees, much less ensure that the committees function meaningfully. The vigilance committees form the core of act enforcement—if implemented as intended, these committees could contribute dramatically to the eradication of bonded labor. For overburdened district collectors, they would provide resources; for corrupt district collectors, they would provide oversight; and for all district collectors, they would provide essential liaison possibilities to the bonded laborer population, whose interests are usually at odds with the interest and sympathies of their local leaders.[337]

Nonetheless, notwithstanding the act's unambiguous requirement that vigilance committees be formed and active, as well as numerous supreme court rulings emphasizing the importance of the committees for act enforcement, Human Rights Watch has learned of no functioning vigilance committee anywhere in India.

Apathy, or at least a low prioritization of child and bonded labor issues, is also evident in the slow pace at which complaints are adjudicated—enforcement in the courts is very slow. One attorney told us of a case he filed with the Supreme Court under the Bonded Labour System (Abolition) Act in 1984. A fact finding committee was not appointed until 1991 and, although arguments and submissions

---

[336] Human Rights Watch telephone interview with Belgian journalist Rudi Rotthier, October 19, 1995.

[337] The Supreme Court noted this in directing states to include social action groups in their efforts against bonded labor, stating that "patwaris and tehsildars [local leaders] [are] either in sympathy with the exploiting class or lacking in social commitment or indifferent to the misery and suffering of the poor . ." Crim. Writ Petition No. 1263 of 1982, *Neeraja Chaudhary v. State of Madhya Pradesh*, 3 SCC paragraphs 243, 251 (1984).

before the court concluded in 1994, as of 1996 no decision had yet been issued.[338] The time table is not much better for the bonded labor case before the Supreme Court, *People's Union for Civil Liberties v. State of Tamil Nadu, et al.*, which was filed in 1985 and as of 1996 was under consideration by the court.

Delays in prosecuting cases under the Child Labour (Prohibition and Regulation) Act are also not uncommon. One such case, filed in 1986 shortly after the act took effect, was reported to be still pending at the prosecution stage eight years later, in 1994, with the accused continuing to engage in prohibited practices. The delay in processing the complaint, filed against an owner of a glass and bangles factory in Firozabad, is all the more startling in view of the fact that the complaint was filed by then-Labour Minister P. A. Sangma.[339]

### Caste and Class Bias

A key element of enforcement is the attitude and the tendency toward a subjective interpretation of the Bonded Labour System (Abolition) Act, 1976 by government officials, including district magistrates, police officers, labor inspectors, and judges. Too often, because of their own backgrounds and the climate in which they work, those officers entrusted with enforcement are more sympathetic to the employers than to the child or bonded laborers. This phenomenon has been noted repeatedly in the context of enforcement of the Bonded Labour System (Abolition) Act.

> We had some time back a case before us where pursuant to a direction given by the Collector as a result of an order made by this Court, the Tehsildar went to the villages in question and sitting on a dais with the landlords by his side, he started enquiring of the labourers whether they were bonded or not and when the labourers, obviously inhibited and terrified by the presence of the landlords, said that they were not bonded but they were working freely and voluntarily, he made a report to the Collector that there were no bonded labourers.[340]

---

[338] Human Rights Watch interview with attorney Jose Varghese, November 15, 1996, New Delhi.

[339] *Child Workers News*, Vol. 2, No. 2, April-June 1994.

[340] Crim. Writ Petition No. 1263 of 1982, *Neeraja Chaudhary v. State of Madhya Pradesh*, 3 SCC 243, paragraph 252 (1984).

In the rare instances where vigilance committees or similar bodies have been formed, according to one researcher, they have been composed of people who themselves, either directly or through their families, employ bonded labor.[341] District collectors and other civil servants assigned to bonded labor enforcement are also more often than not aligned with the property-holding—including the holding of bonded laborers—class. One researcher told Human Rights Watch of working with a team of three Indian Administrative Service officers, who had been assigned by the Supreme Court to investigate a case of bonded labor affecting between 2,500 and 3,000 people. The investigators were urban middle-class men from land-owning families in the region; in private conversations, they made it clear that they considered the use of bonded labor to be an acceptable practice.[342]

Many bond masters are themselves government employees, including teachers, railway workers, and civil administrators.[343] Because of their steady income, these people are more likely to own land—which they need someone to cultivate—and are more likely to have money available for lending purposes. They are also more likely to be local leaders and to have ties to the local and district administration, both factors which tend to inhibit prosecution.

Despite the obvious limitations of relying on high-caste and local landowning officials to attack bonded labor, outreach by the government to affected populations and collaboration with grass-roots social actions groups have not yet been implemented to any significant degree.

**Obstruction**

It is not uncommon for those accused of violating labor laws to engage in overt obstruction of the legal process. This ranges from intimidation of the

---

[341] Tiwary, "Bondage in Santhal Parganas," *Chains of Servitude*, p. 207.

[342] "Bonded labour is employed by powerful landlords from whom the many political parties draw political support and this poses a major obstacle to implementation of the legislation. The power of those opposed to the eradication of bondage ensures the continuation of the economic conditions which nurture the system." See Mahajan and Gathia, *Child Labour: An Analytical Study*, p. 25.

[343] Human Rights Watch interviews with local social activists, December 1, 1995, Trichy, Tamil Nadu, and December 18, 1995, Varanasi, Uttar Pradesh.

complaining workers, to bribery of government officials, to physical threats and violence against the bonded laborers and their advocates.[344]

Those who file suit against employers of bonded labor are frequently harassed, according to a New Delhi lawyer who has been engaged in bonded labor cases for more than a decade.[345]

The danger is greatest to those who work in rural areas, where bondage is often the norm and is employed by powerful and ruthless owners. According to another attorney closely related to bonded labor litigation, the advocates and especially the workers who complain about their status are "risking their lives... they are putting their lives on the line, and the state officials have turned a callous eye to it."[346]

Government officials may do more than just turn a "callous eye" toward violence against the bonded laborers and their advocates. Several activists told Human Rights Watch of police collusion with local employers, including returning escaped workers to the employers and intimidating, through force or threat of force, workers who are attempting to organize for improved conditions.[347]

### Corruption

As noted in previous chapters, corruption among government officials charged with enforcement of labor laws is notorious and widespread. Labor inspectors, medical officers, local tehsildars (representatives of the district magistrates at the local level), and judges and judicial magistrates are all known to be susceptible to bribery.

### Lack of Accountability

Under the Bonded Labour System (Abolition) Act, district magistrates are supposed to report to the state government periodically regarding the number of cases of bonded laborers identified, released, and rehabilitated. Most district

---

[344] These phenomena are discussed in previous chapters.

[345] Human Rights Watch interview with Jose Varghese, November 15, 1995, New Delhi.

[346] Human Rights Watch interview with Supreme Court attorney, December 29, 1996.

[347] For example, see Ajoy Kumar, "From Slavery to Freedom: The Tale of Chattisgarh Bonded Labourers," Indian Social Institute, 1986, pp. 12-13.

magistrates either do not make these reports at all, or make them sporadically. Furthermore, no mechanism is in place whereby the accuracy of the district-level reports can be ascertained, including such important issues as how many of the identified workers have actually been released, and whether any released workers have relapsed into bondage. Often, the district magistrates will simply report that identified bonded laborers, or formerly released bonded laborers, are "unavailable for rehabilitation." That is to say, that their whereabouts are unknown. Hence the central government's figures for 1994-1995, which state that, of 251,424 bonded labourers identified between 1976 and 1995, 17,127 are "not available for rehabilitation."[348]

The rate of return into bondage by previously released bonded laborers is neither studied nor recorded by the government; the effectiveness of the rehabilitation scheme is therefore unknown. Various nongovernmental sources believe the relapse rate to be very high.[349] Part of the reason for return may be the long delays between identification of bonded laborers and dispersal of rehabilitation monies to them.[350] Another factor may be the reportedly widespread corruption among enforcing officials, who are accused of siphoning off funds earmarked for rehabilitation purposes.

### Lack of Adequate Enforcement Staff

Yet another obstacle to enforcement is the failure to devote sufficient resources to the issue of bonded child labor. This failure includes inadequate training of labor inspectors, an insufficient number of inspectors,[351] and an

---

[348] Ministry of Labour, *Annual Report 1994-1995*, p. 97.

[349] See G. Satyamurty, "Trouble Dogs Freed Bonded Labourers," *The Hindu*, October 27, 1994; also, in a memorandum to Human Rights Watch, journalists Marleen Daniels and Rudi Rotthier reported their discovery in a rural village that, of twenty-one children liberated from bondage in 1993, nineteen had been returned to bondage one year later. (Rotthier/Daniels memorandum to Human Rights Watch, November 1, 1995).

[350] For example, in Tamil Nadu, the rehabilitation allowance for a bonded laborer released in December 1992 was not approved for distribution until March 1994. Report of the Commission on Bonded Labour in Tamil Nadu, October 31, 1995, Madras, submitted in connection with Supreme Court Civ. Writ Petition No. 3922 of 1985, p. 18.

[351] See Commission on Labour Standards and International Trade, *Child Labour in India...*, p. 40.

overburdening of the district magistrates.[352] At both the state and the district level, the number of personnel devoted to enforcement of child and bonded labor laws is blatantly inadequate. In Tamil Nadu, for example, "there is only one Assistant Section Officer dealing with the bonded labour issue for the whole State... [and he] also holds other responsibilities.[353]

---

[352] See *Neeraja Chaudhary v. State of Madhya Pradesh*, paragraph 251.

[353] Report of the Commission on Bonded Labour in Tamil Nadu, October 31, 1995, Madras, submitted in connection with Supreme Court Civ. Writ Petition No. 3922 of 1985, p. 137.

# VII. CONCLUSION: COMBATING BONDED CHILD LABOR

The eradication of bonded child labor in India depends on the Indian government's commitment to two imperatives: enforcement of the Bonded Labour System (Abolition) Act, and the creation of meaningful alternatives for already-bonded child laborers and those at risk of joining their ranks.

In addition to genuine government action, it is essential that nongovernmental organizations be encouraged by the government to collaborate in this effort. The government has the resources and authority to implement the law, while community-based organizations have the grass-roots contacts and trust necessary to facilitate this implementation. Furthermore, nongovernmental groups can act as a watchdog on government programs, keeping vigil for corruption, waste, and apathy. The elimination of current debt bondage and the prevention of new or renewed bondage therefore requires a combination of concerted government action and extensive community involvement. Neither standing alone is sufficient. Bonded labor is a vast, pernicious, and long-standing social ill, and the tenacity of the bonded labor system must be attacked with similar tenacity; anything less than total commitment is certain to fail.

## ENFORCEMENT OF THE BONDED LABOUR SYSTEM (ABOLITION) ACT

The Bonded Labour System (Abolition) Act was passed into law in 1976. Twenty years later, Human Rights Watch has found that the goals of this law—to punish employers of bonded labor and to identify, release, and rehabilitate bonded laborers—have not been met, and efforts to do so are sporadic and weak at best. The bonded labor system continues to thrive.

The district-level vigilance committees, mandated by the Bonded Labour System (Abolition) Act and constituting the key tool of act enforcement, have not been formed in most districts. Those that have formed tend to lie dormant, or, worse yet, are comprised of members unsympathetic to the plight of bonded laborers, in direct contravention of Supreme Court orders interpreting the act.

Without effective vigilance committees to assist, guide, and oversee their efforts, district collectors are left alone in their efforts to enforce the law. Collectors interested in enforcement are limited in these efforts by competing administrative and prosecutorial duties; without vigilance committees to share the work, meaningful enforcement of the Bonded Labour System (Abolition) Act is difficult. Other collectors are not interested in enforcing the act; for them, the lack of a good vigilance committee means there is no pressure to do so.

Whether for lack of will or lack of support, India's district collectors have failed utterly to enforce the provisions of the Bonded Labour System (Abolition)

145

Act. If collected statistics regarding prosecutions under the act after 1988 exist, Human Rights Watch was unable to obtain them. The only attempted prosecutions we learned of occurred in Tamil Nadu in 1995, when eight employers of bonded child labor were arrested, kept in jail over night, and fined a nominal amount. The state of Tamil Nadu has an estimated one million bonded laborers; according to the North Arcot District Collector, these were the first charges ever brought under the act in Tamil Nadu.

In addition to prosecuting violators, district collectors are directed by the act to identify, release, and rehabilitate bonded laborers. India has an estimated fifteen million bonded child laborers alone. The Indian government's Ministry of Labour, however, estimated in 1995 that there were just 2,784 bonded laborers of all ages identified and awaiting rehabilitation. It made no mention of any bonded laborers yet to be identified. Non-enforcement of the law is virtually guaranteed, of course, so long as the government engages in a willful denial regarding the existence and pervasiveness of bonded labor.

The mandated rehabilitation of released workers is essential. Without adequate rehabilitation, those who are released will quickly fall again into bondage. This has been established repeatedly, among both adult and child bonded laborers. Nonetheless, the central and state governments have jointly failed to implement required rehabilitation procedures. Rehabilitation allowances are distributed late, or are not distributed at all, or are paid out at half the proper rate, with corrupt officials pocketing the difference. One government-appointed commission found that court orders mandating the rehabilitation of bonded laborers were routinely ignored.[354]

Finally, the Bonded Labour System (Abolition) Act directs vigilance committees and district collectors to institute savings and credit programs at the community level, so that the impoverished might have access to a small loan during financial emergencies. This resource is crucial. Just as enforcement of the law against employers would work to terminate the demand for bonded labor, so would available credit work to end the supply. Nearly every child interviewed by Human Rights Watch told the same story: they were sold to their employers because their parents were desperate for money and had no other way to get it. For some, it was the illness or death of a parent, for others, the marriage of a sister, and for others still, the need to buy food or put a roof over their heads. In most cases, the amount of the debt incurred was very small.

---

[354] Sreedhar Pillai, "Of Inhuman Bondage: The Supreme Court Indicts the Tamil Nadu Government for Failing to Abolish Bonded Labour," *Sunday Magazine* (Calcutta), April 7-13, 1996.

A community-based savings and credit program has been introduced in North Arcot district, and early indications are that it will strike a significant blow against bonded child labor. The program was launched by the district collector for North Arcot, who claimed that sufficient funds and personnel were available from existing rural development programs. Similar initiatives should be instituted in all areas where bonded child labor is prevalent.

## CREATING ALTERNATIVES TO BONDED CHILD LABOR

Bonded child labor must be attacked from many fronts. Enforcement of the law is essential, but it is not enough. The bonded child laborer must have someplace else to go. The child's parents must have other options available. The community must support the end of debt bondage for children. In sum, the attack must be holistic—it must work to change the *system* of debt bondage. Elements already in use by community activists and some government officials include: education, including vocational training and popular education, and rural development.

The availability of free, compulsory, and quality education is widely regarded as the single most important factor in the fight against bonded and non-bonded child labor. The correlation between illiteracy and bonded labor is strong, with researchers reporting that literacy rates among bonded child laborers are as low as 5 percent.[355] The majority of children interviewed by Human Rights Watch had been schooled for three years or less, and many said they could not read or write.

Article 45 of the Indian Constitution commits the state to "endeavor[ing] to provide, within a period of ten years from the commencement of this Constitution, for free and compulsory education for all children until they complete the age of fourteen years." The constitution came into force in 1950. Recognizing the central importance of education, India's leading non-governmental organizations have called for the implementation of universal, free, and compulsory education. Among them are: the Child Labour Action Network (CLAN), the Campaign Against Child Labour (CACL), the Centre for Rural Education and Development Action (CREDA), and the Bonded Labour Liberation Front (BLLF). UNICEF-India and Anti-Slavery International have likewise called on the Indian government to implement education for all.

At the same time, alternate efforts to at least minimally educate bonded children are already underway in a few areas. CREDA in the carpet-belt, the MV Foundation in Andhra Pradesh, and the Indian Council on Child Welfare (ICCW)

---

[355] Tiwary, "Bondage in Santhal Parganas," *Chains of Servitude...*, p. 205.

in North Arcot, are all involved in non-formal education initiatives. Some of these programs utilize modest financial support to attract children, including small cash stipends and periodic grain allowances. In addition to classic schooling, children on the verge of adulthood may benefit from concrete skills training as well.

CREDA and the MV Foundation also emphasize popular education for all members of the community, in which community teachers stress the importance of education for children and the deleterious effects of exploitative child labor. Such outreach to the community as a whole is necessary in order to chip away at the thick web of myths and justifications that support the exploitation of child workers. These myths contend that children must be trained at the "right" age or they will never learn a skill; children must be trained in a profession "appropriate" to their caste and background; children are well-suited for certain kinds of work because of their "nimble fingers;" and child labor is a natural and inevitable function of the family unit. These views are widely shared by parents, educators, government officials, and the public at large, with the result that talk of children's rights in regard to labor is dismissed summarily. It is necessary to change these views in order to change the system.

In sum, the fight against bonded child labor must be carried out on two fronts: enforcement and prevention. Those employers who continue to bind children to them with debt, paying just pennies for a hazardous and grueling work day, must be prosecuted under the Bonded Labour System (Abolition) Act. Employers or agents that physically abuse, kidnap, unlawfully confine, threaten with violence, or expose to dangerous conditions, within the context of the bonded labor system, should be prosecuted for these crimes under the Indian Penal Code and the Juvenile Justice Act, 1986. Children must be removed from bondage and rehabilitated to avoid a subsequent return to bondage. Finally, the educational and survival needs of all children at risk must be addressed in order to stop the cycle of bondage.

# APPENDICES

## APPENDIX A: Selected Articles of the Indian Constitution

**Article 21. Protection of life and personal liberty**—No person shall be deprived of his life or personal liberty except according to procedure established by law.

**Article 23. Prohibition of traffic in human beings and forced labour**—(1) Traffic in human beings and begar and other similar forms of forced labour are prohibited and any contravention of this prohibition shall be an offence punishable in accordance with law.
(2) Nothing in this article shall prevent the State from imposing compulsory service for public purposes, and in imposing such service the State shall not make any discrimination on grounds only of religion, race, caste or class or any of them.

**Article 24. Prohibition of employment of children in factories, etc.**—No child below the age of fourteen years shall be employed to work in any factory or mine or engaged in any other hazardous employment.

**Article 39. Certain principles of policy to be followed by the State**—The State shall, in particular, direct its policy towards securing—
    (a) that the citizens, men and women equally, have the right to an adequate means of livelihood;
    (b) that the ownership and control of the material resources of the community are so distributed as best to subserve the common good;
    (c) that the operation of the economic system does not result in the concentration of wealth and means of production to the common detriment;
    (d) that there is equal pay for equal work for both men and women;
    (e) that the health and strength of workers, men and women, and the tender age of children are not abused and that citizens are not forced by economic necessity to enter avocations unsuited to their age or strength;
    (f) that children are given opportunities and facilities to develop in a healthy manner and in conditions of freedom and dignity and that childhood and youth are protected against exploitation and against moral and material abandonment.

**Article 39A. Equal Justice and free legal aid**—The State shall secure that the operation of the legal system promotes justice, on a basis of equal opportunity, and shall, in particular, provide free legal aid, by suitable legislation or schemes or in any other way, to ensure that opportunities for securing justice are not denied to any citizen by reason of economic or other disabilities.

**Article 41. Right to work, to education and to public assistance in certain cases**—The State shall, within the limits of its economic capacity and development, make effective provision for securing the right to work, to education and to public assistance in cases of unemployment, old age, sickness and disablement, and in other cases of undeserved want.

**Article 42. Provision for just and humane conditions of work and maternity relief**—The State shall make provision for securing just and humane conditions of work and for maternity relief.

**Article 43. Living wage, etc., for workers**—The State shall endeavour to secure, by suitable legislation or economic organisation or in any other way, to all workers, agricultural, industrial or otherwise, work, a living wage, conditions of work ensuring a decent standard of life and full enjoyment of leisure and social and cultural opportunities and, in particular, the State shall endeavour to promote cottage industries on an individual or cooperative basis in rural areas.

**Article 43A. Participation of workers in management of industries**—The State shall take steps, by suitable legislation or in any other way, to secure the participation of workers in the management of undertakings, establishments or other organizations engaged in any industry.

**Article 45. Provision for free and compulsory education for children**—The State shall endeavour to provide within a period of ten years from the commencement of this Constitution, for free and compulsory education for all children until they complete the age of fourteen years.

**Article 46. Promotion of educational and economic interests of Scheduled Castes, Scheduled Tribes and other weaker sections**—The State shall promote with special care the educational and economic interests of the weaker sections of the people, and, in particular, of the Scheduled Castes and the Scheduled Tribes, and shall protect them from social injustice and all forms of exploitation.

## APPENDIX B: The Bonded Labour System (Abolition) Act, 1976
### (No. 19 of 1976)

**[9th February, 1976]**

*An act to provide for the abolition of bonded labour system with a view to preventing the economic and physical exploitation of the weaker sections of the people and for matters connected therewith or incidental thereto*

Be it enacted by Parliament in the Twenty-seventh Year of the Republic of India as follows:

### CHAPTER I
### Preliminary

**1. Short title, extent and commencement.**—(1) This act may be called the Bonded Labour System (Abolition) Act, 1976.

(2) It extends to the whole of India.

(3) it shall be deemed to have come into force on the 25th day of October, 1975.

**2. Definitions.—(1) In This act, unless the context otherwise requires,—**

(a) "advance" means an advance, whether in cash or in kind, or partly in cash or partly in kind, made by one person (hereinafter referred to as the creditor) to another person (hereinafter referred to as the debtor);

(b) "agreement" means an agreement (whether written or oral, or partly written and partly oral) between a debtor and creditor, and includes an agreement providing for forced labour, the existence of which is presumed under any social custom prevailing in the concerned locality;

*Explanation.*—The existence of an agreement between the debtor and creditor is ordinarily presumed, under the social custom, in relation to the following forms of forced labour, namely:

Adiyamar, Baramasi, Bethu, Bhagela, Cherumar, Garrugalu, Hali, Hari, Harwai, Holya, Jolya, Jeeta, Kamiya, Khundit-Mundit, Kuthia, Lakhari, Munjhi, Mat, Musish system, Nit-Majoor, Paleru, Padiyal, Pannaayilal, Sagri, Sanji, Sanjawal, Sewak,, Sewakis, Seri, Vetti;

151

(c) "ascendant" or "descendant" in relation to a person belonging to matriarchal society, means the person who corresponds to such expression in accordance with the law of succession in such society;

(d) "bonded debt" means an advance obtained, or presumed to have been obtained, by a bonded labourer, or in pursuance of, the bonded labour system

(e) "bonded labour" means any labour or service rendered under the bonded labour system;

(f) "bonded labourer" means a labourer who incurs, or has, or is presumed to have, incurred, a bonded debt;

(g) "bonded labour system" means the system of forced, or partly forced labour under which a debtor enters, or has, or is presumed to have, entered, into an agreement with the creditor to the effect that,—

(i) In consideration of an advance obtained by him or by any of his lineal ascendants or descendants (whether or not such advance is evidenced by any document) and in consideration of the interest, if any, due on such advance, or

(ii) in pursuance of any customary or social obligation, or

(iii) in pursuance of an obligation devolving on him by succession, or

(iv) for any economic consideration of the interest, if any, due on such advance, or

(v) by reason of his birth in any particular caste or community, he would—

(1) render, by himself or through any member of his family, or any person dependent on him, labour or service to the creditor, or for the benefit of the creditor, for a specified period or for an unspecified period, either without wages or for nominal wages, or

(2) forfeit the freedom of employment or other means of livelihood for a specified period or for an unspecified period, or

(3) forfeit the right to move freely throughout the territory of India, or

(4) forfeit the right to appropriate or sell at market value any of his property or product of his labour or the labour of a member of his family or any person dependent on him

and includes the system of forced, or partly forced, labour under which a surety for a debtor or has, or has, or is presumed to have, entered, into an agreement with the creditor to the effect that in the event of the failure of the debtor to repay the debt, he would render the bonded labour on behalf of the debtor;

> *Explanation.—* For the removal of doubts, it is hereby declared that any system of forced, or partly forced labour under which any workman being contract labour as defined in Cl. (b) of subsection (1) or Sec. 2 of the Contract Labour (Regulation and Abolition) Act, 1970 (37 of 1970), or an inter-State migrant workman as defined in Cl. (e) of sub-section (1) of Sec. 2 of the Inter-State Migrant Workmen (Regulation and of Employment and Conditions of Service) Act, 1979 (30 of 1979), is required to render labour or service in circumstances of the nature mentioned in sub-clause (1) of this clause or is subjected to all or any of the disabilities referred to in sub-clauses (2) to (4), is "bonded labour system" within the meaning of this clause.

(h) "family", in relation to a person, includes the ascendant and descendant of such person;

(i) "nominal wages", in relation to any labour, means a wage which is less than,—

> (a) the minimum wages fixed by the Government, in relation to the same or similar labour, under any law for the time being in force; and
> (b) where no such minimum wage has been fixed in relation to any form of labour, the wages that are normally paid, for the same or similar labour to the labourers working in the same locality;

(j) "prescribed" means prescribed by rules made under this act.

**3. Act to have overriding effect.**—The provisions of this act shall have effect notwithstanding anything inconsistent therewith contained in any enactment other than this act, or in any instrument having effect by virtue of any enactment other than this act.

## CHAPTER II
### Abolition of Bonded Labour System

**4. Abolition of bonded labour system.**—(1) On the commencement of this act, the bonded labour system shall stand abolished and every bonded labourer shall, on such commencement, stand freed and discharged from any obligation to render any bonded labour.

(2) After the commencement of this act, no person shall—

(a) make any advance under, or in pursuance of the bonded labour system, forced labour, or

(b) Compel any person to render any bonded labour or other form of forced labour.

**5. Agreement, custom, etc. to be void.**—On the commencement of this act, any custom or tradition or any contract, agreement or other instrument (whether entered into or executed before or after the commencement of this act), by virtue of which any person, or any member of the family or dependent of such person, is required to do any work or render any service as a bonded labourer, shall be void and inoperative.

## CHAPTER III
### Extinguishment of liability to repay bonded debt

**6.   Liability to repay bonded debt to stand extinguished**—(1) On the commencement of this act, every obligation of a bonded labourer to repay any bonded debt, or such part of any bonded debt as remains unsatisfied immediately before such commencement, shall be deemed to have been extinguished.

(2) After the commencement of this act, no suit or other proceeding shall lie in any civil Court or before any other authority for the recovery of any bonded debt or any part thereof.

(3) Every decree or order for the recovery of bonded debt, passed before the commencement of this act and not fully satisfied before such commencement, shall be deemed, on such commencement, to have been fully satisfied.

(4) Every attachment made before the commencement of this act, for the recovery of any bonded debt, shall, on such commencement, stand vacated; and where, in pursuance of such attachment, any moveable property of the bonded labourer was seized and removed from his custody and kept in the custody of any Court or other authority pending sale thereof such moveable property shall be restored, as soon as may be practicable after such commencement, to the possession of the bonded labourer.

(5) Where, before the commencement of this act, possession of any property belonging to a bonded labourer or a member of his family or other dependent was forcibly taken over by any creditor for the recovery of any bonded debt, such property shall be restored, as soon as may be practicable after such commencement, to the possession of the person from whom it was seized.

(6) If restoration of the possession of any property referred to in sub-section (4) or sub-section (5) is not made within thirty days from the commencement of this act, the aggrieved person may, within such time as may be prescribed, apply to the prescribed authority for the restoration of the possession of such property and the prescribed authority may, after giving the creditor a reasonable opportunity of being heard, direct the creditor to restore to the applicant the possession of the concerned property within such time as may be specified in the order.

(7) An order made by any prescribed authority, under sub-section (6), shall be deemed to be an order made by a civil Court of the lowest pecuniary jurisdiction within the local limits of whose jurisdiction the creditor voluntarily resides or carries on business or personally works for gain.

(8) For the avoidance of doubts, it is hereby declared, that, where any attached property was sold before the commencement of this act, in execution of a decree or order for the recovery of a bonded debt, such sale shall not be affected by any provision of this act:

Provided that the bonded labourer, or an agent authorized by him in this behalf, may, at any time within five years rom such commencement, apply to have the sale set aside on his depositing in Court, for payment to the decree-holder, the amount specified in the proclamation of sale, for the recovery of which sale was ordered, less any amount as well as mesne profits, which may, since the date of such proclamation of sale, have been received by the decree-holder.

(9) Where any suit or proceeding, for the enforcement of any obligation under the bonded labour system, including a suit or proceeding for the recovery of any advance made to a bonded labourer, is pending at the commencement of this act, such suit or other proceeding shall, on such commencement, stand dismissed.

(10) On the commencement of this act, every bonded labourer who has been detained in civil prison, whether before or after judgement, shall be released from detention forthwith.

**7. Property of bonded labourer to be freed from mortgage, etc.**—(1) All property vested in a bonded labourer which was, immediately before the commencement of this act under any mortgage, lien, charge, or other incumbrances in connection with any bonded debt shall, in so far as it is relatable to the bonded debt, stand freed and discharged from such mortgage, charge, lien or other incumbrances in connection with any bonded debt, and where any such property was, immediately before the commencement of this act, in the possession of the mortgagee or the holder of the charge, lien or incumbrance, such property shall (except where it was subject to any other charge), on such commencement, be restored to the possession of the bonded labourer.

(2) If any delay is made in restoring any property, referred to in sub-section (1), to the possession of the bonded labourer, such labourer shall be entitled, on and from the date of such commencement, to recover from the mortgagee or holder of the lien, charge or incumbrance, such mesne profits as may be determined by the Civil Court of the lowest pecuniary jurisdiction within the local limits of whose jurisdiction such property is situated.

**8. Freed bonded labourer not to be evicted from homestead, etc.**— (1) No person who has been freed and discharged under this act from any obligation to render any bonded labour, shall be evicted from any homestead or other residential premises which he was occupying immediately before the commencement of this act as part of the consideration for the bonded labour.

(2) If, after the commencement of this act, any such person is evicted by the creditor from any homestead or other residential premises, referred to in sub-section (1), the Executive Magistrate in charge of the sub-division within which such homestead or residential premises, is situated shall, as early as practicable, restore the bonded labourer to the possession of such homestead or other residential premises.

**9. Creditor not to accept payment against extinguished debt.**—(1) No creditor shall accept any payment against any bonded debt which has been extinguished or deemed to have been extinguished or fully satisfied by virtue of the provisions of this act.

(2) whoever contravenes the provisions of sub-section (1), shall be punishable with imprisonment for a term which may extend to three years and also with fine.

(3) The Court, convicting any person under sub-section (2) may, in addition to the penalties which may be imposed under that sub-section, direct the person to deposit, in Court, the amount accepted in contravention of the provisions of sub-section (1), within such period as may be specified in the order for being refunded to the bonded labourer.

## CHAPTER IV
### Implementing Authorities

**10. Authorities who may be specified for implementing the provisions of this act.**— The State Governments may confer such powers and impose such duties on a District Magistrate as may be necessary to ensure that the provisions of this act are properly carried out and the District Magistrate may specify the officer, subordinate to him, who shall exercise all or any of the powers, and perform al or any of the duties, so conferred or imposed and the local limits within which such powers or duties shall be carried out by the officers so specified.

**11. Duty of District Magistrates and other officers to ensure credit.**—The District Magistrate authorized by the State Government under Sec. 10 and the officer specified by the District Magistrate under that section shall, as far as practicable, try to promote the welfare of the freed bonded labourer by securing and protecting the economic interests of such bonded labourer so that he may not have any occasion or reason to contract any further debt.

**12. Duty of the District Magistrate and officers authorized by him.**—It shall be the duty of every District Magistrate and every officer specified by him under Sec. 10 to inquire whether after the commencement of this act, any bonded labour system or any other form of forced labour is being enforced by, or on behalf of, any person resident within the local limits of his jurisdiction and if, as a result of such inquiry, any person is found to be enforcing the bonded labour system or any other system of forced labour, he shall forthwith take such action as may be necessary to eradicate the enforcement of such forced labour.

## CHAPTER V
### Vigilance Committees

**13. Vigilance Committees.**—(1) Every State Government shall, by notification in the Official Gazette, constitute such number of Vigilance Committees in each district and each sub-division as it may think fit.

(2) Each Vigilance Committee, constituted for a district, shall consist of the following members, namely:

(a) The District Magistrate, or a person nominated by him, who shall be the Chairman;

(b) three persons belonging to the Scheduled Castes or Scheduled Tribes and residing in the district, to be nominated by the District Magistrate;

(c)  two social workers, resident in the district, to be nominated by the District Magistrate;

(d) not more than three persons to represent the official or non-official agencies in the district connected with rural development, to be nominated by the State Government;

(e) one person to represent the financial and credit institutions in the district, to be nominated by the District Magistrate.

(3) Each Vigilance Committee, constituted for a sub-division, shall consist of the following members, namely:

(a) The Sub-Divisional Magistrate, or a person nominated by him, who shall be the Chairman;

(b) three persons belonging to the Scheduled Castes or Scheduled Tribes and residing in the sub-division, to be nominated by the Sub-divisional Magistrate;

(c)  two social workers, resident in the sub-division, to be nominated by the Sub-divisional Magistrate;

(d) not more than three persons to represent the official or non-official agencies in the sub-division connected with rural development, to be nominated by the State Government;

(e) one person to represent the financial and credit institutions in the sub-division, to be nominated by the Sub-divisional Magistrate.

(f) one officer specified under Sec. 10 and functioning in the sub-division;

(4) Each Vigilance Committee shall regulate its own procedure and secretarial assistance as may be necessary, shall be provided by—

(a) the District Magistrate, in the case of Vigilance Committee constituted for the district;

(b) the Sub-divisional Magistrate, in the case of a Vigilance Committee constituted for the sub-division.

(5) No proceeding of a Vigilance Committee shall be invalid merely by reason of any defect in the constitution, or in the proceedings, of the Vigilance Committee.

**14. Functions of Vigilance Committees.**—(1) The functions of each Vigilance Committee shall be—

(a) to advise the District Magistrate or any officer authorized by him as to the efforts made, and action taken, to ensure that the provisions of this act or any rule made thereunder are properly implemented;

(b) to provide for the economic and social rehabilitation of the freed-bonded labourers;

(c) to co-ordinate the functions of rural banks and co-operative societies with a view to canalizing adequate credit to the freed-bonded labourers;

(d) to keep an eye on the number of offences of which cognizance has been taken under this act;

(e) to make a survey as to whether there is any offence of which cognizance ought to be taken under this act;

(f) to defend any suit instituted against a freed-bonded labourer or a member of his family or any other person dependent on him for the recovery of the whole or part of any bonded debt or any other debt which is claimed by such person to be bonded debt.

(2) A Vigilance Committee may authorize one of its members to defend a suit against a freed-bonded labourer and the member so authorized shall be deemed, for the purpose of such suit, to be the authorized agent of the freed-bonded labourer.

**15. Burden of proof.**— Whenever any debt is claimed by a bonded labourer, or a Vigilance Committee, to be a bonded debt, the burden of proof that such debt, is not a bonded debt shall lie on the creditor.

## CHAPTER VI
### Offences and Procedure for Trial

**16. Punishment for enforcement of bonded labour.**—Whoever, after the commencement of this act, compels any person to render any bonded labour shall be punishable with imprisonment for a term which may extend to three years and also with fine which may extend to two thousand rupees.

**17. Punishment for advancement of bonded debt.**—Whoever advances, after the commencement of this act, any bonded debt shall be punishable with imprisonment for a term which may extend to three years and also with fine which may extend to two thousand rupees.

**18. Punishment for extracting bonded labour under the bonded labour system.**—Whoever enforces, after the commencement of this act, any custom, tradition, contract, agreement or other instrument, by virtue of which any person or any member of the family of such person or any dependent of such person is required to render any service under the bonded labour system shall be punishable with imprisonment for a term which may extend to three years and also with fine which may extend to two thousand rupees; and out of the fine, if recovered, payment shall be made to the bonded labourer at the rate of rupees five for each day for which the bonded labour was extracted from him.

**19. Punishment for omission or failure to restore possession of property to bonded labourers.**—Whoever, being required by this act to restore any property to the possession of any bonded labourer, omits or fails to do so, within a period of thirty days from the commencement of this act, shall be punishable with imprisonment for a term which may extend to one year, or with fine which may extend to one thousand rupees, or with both; and, out of the fine, if recovered payment shall be made to the bonded labourer at the rate of rupees five for each day during which possession of property was not restored to him.

**20. Abetment to be an offence.**—Whoever abets any offence punishable under this act shall, whether or not the offence abetted is committed, be punishable with the same punishment as is provided for the offence which has been abetted.

> *Explanation.*—For the purpose of this act, "abetment" has the meaning assigned to it in the Indian Penal Code.

**21. Offences to be tried by Executive Magistrates.**—(1) The State Government may confer, on an Executive Magistrate the powers of a Judicial Magistrate of the first class or of the second class for the trial of offences under this act; and on such conferment of powers, the Executive Magistrate, on whom the powers are so conferred, shall be deemed, for the purposes of the Code of Criminal Procedure, 1973 (2 of 1974), to be a Judicial Magistrate of the first class, or of the second class, as the case may be.

**22. Cognizance of offences.**—Every offence under this act shall be cognizable and bailable.

**23. Offences by companies.**—(1) Where an offence under this act has been committed by a company, every person who, at the time the offence was committed, was in charge of, and was responsible to, the company for the conduct of the business of the company, as well as the company, shall be deemed to be guilty of the offence and shall be liable to be proceeded against and punished accordingly.

(2) Notwithstanding anything contained in sub-section (1), where any offence under this act has been committed by a company and it has been proved that the offence has been committed with the consent or connivance of, or is attributable to, any neglect on the part of, any director, manager, secretary or other officer of the company, such director, manager, secretary or other officer shall be deemed to be guilty of that offence and shall be liable to be proceeded against and punished accordingly.

*Explanation.*—For the purposes of this section,—

(a) "company" means any body corporate and includes a firm or other association of individuals; and

(b) "director", in relation to a firm, means a partner in the firm.

## CHAPTER VII
### Miscellaneous

**24. Protection of action taken in good faith.**—No suit, prosecution or other legal proceeding shall lie against any State Government or any officer of the State Government or any member of the Vigilance Committee for anything which is in good faith done or intended to be done under this act.

**25. Jurisdiction of Civil Courts barred.**—No Civil Court shall have jurisdiction in respect of any matter to which any provision of this act applies and no injunction shall be granted by any Civil Court in respect of anything which is done or intended to be done by or under this act.

**26. Power to make rules.**—(1) The Central Government may, by notification in the official Gazette, make rules for carrying out the provisions of this act.

(2) In particular, and without prejudice to the foregoing power, such rules may provide for all or any of the following matters, namely:

(a) the authority to which application for the restoration of possession of property referred to in sub-section (4), or sub-section (5) of Sec. 6 is to be submitted in pursuance of sub-section (6) of that section;

(b) the time within which application for restoration of possession of property is to be made under sub-section (6) of Sec. 6, to the prescribed authority;

(c) steps to be taken by Vigilance Committees under Cl. (a) of sub-section (1) of Sec. 14, to ensure the implementation of the provisions of this act or of any rule made thereunder;

(d) any other matter which is required to be, or may be prescribed.

(3) Every rule made by the Central Government under this act shall be laid, as soon as may be after it is made, before each House of Parliament while it is in session, for a total period of thirty days which may be comprised in one session or in two or more successive sessions, and if, before the expiry of the session immediately following the session or successive sessions aforesaid, both Houses agree in making any modification in the rule or both Houses agree that the

rule should not be made, the rule shall thereafter have effect only in such modified form or be of no effect, as the case may be; so however, that any such modification or annulment shall be without prejudice to the validity of anything previously done under that rule.

(1) The Bonded Labour System (Abolition) Ordinance, 1975 (17 of 1975), is hereby repealed.

(2) Notwithstanding such repeal, anything or any action taken under the Ordinance (including any notification published, direction of a nomination made, power conferred, duty imposed or officer specified) shall be deemed to have been done or taken under the corresponding provisions of this act.

**APPENDIX C: The Bonded Labour System (Abolition) Rules, 1976**

**(Published in the Gazette of India, Extraordinary, Part II, Section 3(i), February 28, 1976)**

In exercise of powers conferred by sub-section (1), read with sub-section (2) of Sec. 26 of the Bonded Labour System (Abolition) Act, 1976 (19 of 1976), the Central Government hereby makes the following rules, namely:

**1. Short title and commencement.**—(1) These rules may be called the Bonded Labour System (Abolition) Rules, 1976.

(2) They shall come into force on the date of their publication in the official Gazette.

**2. Definitions.**—In these rules, unless the context otherwise requires,—

(a) "Act" means the Bonded Labour System (Abolition) Act, 1976 (19 of 1976);

(b) "District Vigilance Committee: means a Vigilance Committee constituted for a district under sub-section (1) of Sec. 13;

(c) "section" means a section of the act;

(d) "Sub-divisional Vigilance Committee" means a Vigilance Committee constituted for a sub-division under sub-section (1) of Sec. 13.

**3. Term of office, and vacation of seat members of District Vigilance Committees.**—(1) Every member of a District Vigilance Committee, nominated under Cls. (b), (c), (d) and (e) of sub-section (2) of Sec. 13 shall hold office for a period of two years from the date on which his nomination is notified in the official Gazette and shall, on the expiry of the said period, continue to hold office until his successor is nominated and shall also be eligible for re-nomination.

(2) Every member referred to in sub-rule (1), —

(a) may, by giving notice in writing of not less than thirty days to authority which nominated him, resign his office and, on such resignation being accepted or on the expiry of the notice period of 30 days, whichever is earlier, shall be deemed to have vacated his office.

(b) shall be deemed to have vacated his office,—

(I) if he fails to attend three consecutive meetings of the District Vigilance Committee without obtaining leave of the Chairman of such absence:

163

Provided that the authority, which nominated
him, may, if he is satisfied that such member
was prevented by sufficient cause from
attending the three consecutive meetings of
the Committee restore him to membership;
(ii) if he becomes subject to any of the following
disqualifications, namely:
(1) is adjudged insolvent;
(2) is declared to be of unsound
mind by a competent court;
(3) is convicted of an offence which,
in the opinion of the authority which
nominated him, involves moral
turpitude;
(c) may be removed from office, if the authority, which
nominated such member is of the opinion that such member has
ceased to represent the interest to represent which he was
nominated:

Provided that a member shall not be removed
from office under this clause unless a
reasonable opportunity is given to him for
showing cause against such removal.

(3) A member, nominated to fill a casual vacancy shall gold office for
the unexpired portion of the term of his predecessor.

**4. Term of office, and vacation of seat of members of Sub-
divisional Vigilance Committees.**—(1) Every member of a Sub-divisional
Vigilance Committee, nominated under Cls. (b), (c), (d) and (e) of sub-section
(2) of Sec. 13 shall hold office for a period of two years from the date on which
his nomination is notified in the official Gazette and shall, on the expiry of the
said period, continue to hold office until his successor is nominated and shall
also be eligible for re-nomination.

(2) Every member referred to in sub-rule (1), —

(a) may, by giving notice in writing of not less than thirty days
to authority which nominated him, resign his office and, on such
resignation being accepted or on the expiry of the notice period
of 30 days, whichever is earlier, shall be deemed to have vacated
his office.

(b) shall be deemed to have vacated his office,—

(i) if he fails to attend three consecutive meetings of the Sub-divisional Vigilance Committee without obtaining leave of the Chairman of such absence:

Provided that the authority, which nominated him, may, if he is satisfied that such member was prevented by sufficient cause from attending the three consecutive meetings of the Committee restore him to membership;

(ii) if he becomes subject to any of the following disqualifications, namely:

(1) is adjudged insolvent;

(2) is declared to be of unsound mind by a competent court;

(3) is convicted of an offence which, in the opinion of the authority which nominated him, involves moral turpitude;

(c) may be removed from office, if the authority, which nominated such member is of the opinion that such member has ceased to represent the interest to represent which he was nominated:

Provided that a member shall not be removed from office under this clause unless a reasonable opportunity is given to him for showing cause against such removal.

(3) A member, nominated to fill a casual vacancy shall gold office for the unexpired portion of the term of his predecessor.

**5. Prescribed authority under sub-section (6) of Sec.6.**—An application under sub-section (6) of Sec. 6 for restoration of possession of any property referred to in sub-section (4) or sub-section (5) of that section shall be made to the Executive Magistrate, on whom the powers of a Judicial Magistrate of the first class or of the second class have been conferred under sub-section (1) of Sec. 21, and within the local limits of whose jurisdiction the said property is, or the applicant has reason to believe is, situated at the time of making the application:

Provided that where there are two Executive Magistrates, on one of whom the powers of a Judicial Magistrate of the first class and on the other the powers of a Judicial Magistrate of the second class have been conferred under sub-section (1) of Sec. 21 having jurisdiction to entertain the application for restoration of possession of property referred to in sub-rule (1), the application shall be made to the Executive Magistrate on whom the powers of a Judicial Magistrate of the second class have been conferred.

**6. Time within which an application under sub-section (6) is to be made.—**
An application under sub-section (6) of Sec. 6 for restoration of possession of any property referred to in sub-section (4) or sub-section (5) of that section shall be made within a period of ninety days from the date on which these rules come into force.

**7. Records to be maintained by District Vigilance Committees to ensure the implementation of the provisions of the act and rules.**—In order to ensure the implementation of the act and rules, every District Vigilance Committee shall maintain the following registers in respect of freed-bonded labourer with the local limits of its jurisdiction, namely:

(a) a register containing the name and address of freed bonded labourer;

(b) a register containing the statistics relating to the vacation, occupation, and income of every freed-bonded labourer;

(c) a register containing the details of the benefits which the freed-bonded labourers are receiving, including benefits in the form of land, inputs for agriculture, training in handicrafts and allied occupations, loans at differential rates, interest of employment in urban or non-urban areas;

(d) a register containing details of cases under sub-section (6) of Sec. 6, sub-section (2) of Sec. 8, sub-section (2) of Secs. 9, 16, 17, 18, 19, and 20.

# APPENDIX D: The Children (Pedging of Labour) Act, 1933
## (Act No. 2 of 1933)

**[24th February, 1933]**

### An act to prohibit the pledging of labour of children

Whereas it is expedient to prohibit the making of agreements to pledge the labour of children and the employment of children whose labour has been pledged; It is hereby enacted as follows:

**1. Short title, extent and commencement.**—(1) This act may be called the Children (Pledging of Labour) Act, 1933.

(2) It extends to the whole of India

(3) This section and Secs. 2 and 3 shall come into force at once, and the remaining sections of this act shall come into force on the first day of July, 1933.

**2. Definitions.**— In this act, unless there is anything repugnant in the subject or context,—

"an agreement to pledge the labour of a child" means in agreement, written or oral, express or implied, whereby the parent or guardian of a child, in return for any payment or benefit received by him, undertakes to cause or allow the services of the child to be utilized by him, undertakes to cause or allow the services of the child to be utilized in any employment:

Provided that an agreement made without detriment to a child , and not made in consideration of any benefit other than reasonable wages to be paid for the child's services, and terminable at not more than a week's notice, is not an agreement within the meaning of this definition;

"child" means a person who is under the age of fifteen years; and "guardian" includes any person having legal custody of or control over a child.

**3. Agreement contrary to the act to be void.**—An agreement to pledge the labour of a child shall be void.

**4. Penalty for parent or guardian making agreement to pledge the labour of a child.**—Whoever, being the parent or guardian of a child, makes an agreement to pledge the labour of that child, shall be punished with fine which may extend to fifty rupees.

**5. Penalty for making with a parent or guardian agreement to pledge the labour of a child.**—Whoever makes with the parent or guardian of a child shall be punished with fine which may extend to two hundred rupees.

167

**6.    Penalty for employing a child whose labour has been pledged.**—Whoever, knowing or having reason to believe that an agreement has been made to pledge the labour of a child, in furtherance of such agreement employs such child, or permits such child to be employed in any premises or place under his control, shall be punishable with fine which may extend to two hundred rupees.

[23rd December 1986]

### Statement of Objects and Reasons

There are a number of acts which prohibit the employment of children below 14 years and 15 years in certain specified employments. However, there is no procedure laid down in any law for deciding in which employments, occupations or processes the employment of children should be banned. There is also no law to regulate the working conditions of children in most of the employments where they are not prohibited from working and are working under exploitative conditions.

2. This Bill intends to—

(i) ban the employment of children, i.e., those who have not completed their fourteenth year, in specified occupations and processes;

(ii) lay down a procedure to decide modifications to the Schedule of banned occupations or processes;

(iii) regulate the conditions of work of children in employments where they are not prohibited from working;

(iv) lay down enhanced penalties for employment of children in violation of the provisions of this act, and other acts which forbid the employment of children;

(v) to obtain uniformity in the definition of "child" in the related laws.

3. The Bill seeks to achieve the above objects.

*An act to prohibit the engagement of children in certain employments and to regulate the conditions of work of children in certain other employments.*

Be it enacted by Parliament in the Thirty-seventh year of the Republic of India as follows:

## PART I
## PRELIMINARY

**1. Short title, extent and commencement.**—(1) The act may be called the Child Labour (Prohibition and Regulation) Act, 1986.

(2) It extends to the whole of India.

(3) The provisions of this act, other than part III, shall come into force at once, and part III shall come into force on such date as the Central Government

may, by notification in the Official Gazette, appoint, and different dates may be appointed for different states and for different classes of establishments.

  **2. Definitions.**— In this act, unless the context otherwise requires.

  (i) "appropriate Government" means, in relation to an establishment under the control of the Central Government or a railway administration or a major port or a mine or oil field, the Central Government, and in all other cases, the State Government;

  (ii) "child" means a person who has not completed his fourteenth year of age;

  (iii) "day" means a period of twenty-four hours beginning at mid-night;

  (iv) "establishment" includes a shop, commercial establishment, workshop, farm, residential hotel, restaurant, eating house, theatre or other place of amusement or public entertainment;

  (v) "family" in relation to an occupier, means the individual, the wife or husband, as the case may be, of such individual, and their children, brother or sister of such individual;

  (vi) "occupier", in relation to an establishment or a workshop, means the person who has the ultimate control over the affairs of the establishment or workshop;

  (vii) "port authority" means any authority administering a port;

  (viii) "prescribed" means prescribed by rules made under Section 18;

  (ix) "week" means a period of seven days beginning at mid-night on Saturday night or such other night as may be approved in writing for a particular area by the inspector;

  (x) "workshop" means any premises (including the precincts thereof) wherein any industrial process is carried on, but does not include any premises to which the provisions of section 67 of the Factories Act, 1946, for the time being, apply.

## PART II
## PROHIBITION OF EMPLOYMENT OF CHILDREN IN CERTAIN OCCUPATIONS AND PROCESSES

  **3. Prohibition of employment of children in certain occupations and processes.**—No child shall be employed or permitted to work in any of the occupations set forth in Part A of the Schedule or in any workshop wherein any of the processes set forth in Part B of the Schedule is carried on:

  Provided that nothing in this section shall apply to any workshop wherein any process is carried on by the occupier with the aid of his family or to any school established by, or receiving assistance or recognition from, Government.

**4. Power to amend the Schedule.**—The Central Government after giving, by notification in the Official Gazette, not less than three months notice of its intention so to do, may, be like notification, add any occupation or process to the Schedule and thereupon the Schedule shall be deemed to have been amended accordingly.

**5. Child Labour Technical Advisory Committee.**—(1) The Central Government may, by notification in the Official Gazette, constitute an advisory committee to be called the "Child Labour Technical Advisory Committee" (hereafter in this section referred to as the Committee) to advise the Central Government for the purpose of addition of occupations and processes to the Schedule.

(2) The Committee shall consist of a Chairman and such other members not exceeding ten, as may be appointed by the Central Government.

(3) The Committee shall meet as often as it may consider necessary and shall have power to regulate its own procedure.

(4) The Committee may, if it deems necessary so to do, constitute one or more sub-committees, and may appoint any such sub-committee, whether generally or for the consideration of any particular matter, any person who is not a member of the Committee.

(5) The term of office of, the manner of filing casual vacancies in the office of, and the allowances, if any, payable to, the Chairman and other members of the Committee, and the conditions and restrictions subject to which the Committee may appoint any person who is not a member of the Committee as a member of any of its sub-committees shall be such as may be prescribed.

## PART III
## REGULATION OF CONDITIONS OF WORK OF CHILDREN

**6. Application of Part.**—The provisions of this Part shall apply to an establishment or a class of establishments in which none of the occupations or processes referred to in section 3 is carried on.

**7. Hours and period of work.**—(1) No child shall be required or permitted to work in any establishment in excess of such number of hours as may be prescribed for such establishment or class of establishments.

(2) The period of work on each day shall be so fixed that no period shall exceed three hours and that no child shall work for more than three hours before he has had an interval for rest for at least one hour.

(3) The period of work of a child shall be so arranged that inclusive of his interval for rest, under sub-section (2), it shall not be spread over more than six hours, including the time spent in waiting for work on any day.

(4) No child shall be permitted or required to work between 7 p.m. and 8 a.m.

(5) No child shall be required or permitted to work overtime.

**8. Weekly holidays.**—Every child employed in an establishment shall be allowed in each week, a holiday of one whole day, which day shall be specified by the occupier in a notice permanently exhibited in a conspicuous place in the establishment and the day so specified shall not be altered by the occupier more than once in three months.

**9. Notice to Inspector.**—(1) Every occupier in relation to an establishment in which a child was employed or permitted to work immediately before the date of commencement of this act in relation to such establishment shall, within a period of thirty days from such commencement, send to the Inspector within whose local limits the establishment is situated, a written notice containing the following particulars, namely:—

(a) the name and situation of the establishment;

(b) the name of the person in actual management of the establishment;

(c) the address to which communications relating to the establishment should be sent; and

(d) the nature of the occupation or process carried on in the establishment.

(2) Every occupier, in relation to an establishment, who employs, or permits to work, any child after the date of commencement of this act in relation t such establishment, shall, within a period of thirty days from the date of such employment, send to the Inspector within whose local limits the establishment is situated, a written notice containing the particulars as are mentioned in sub-section (1).

*Explanation.*—For the purposes of sub-sections (1) and (2), "date of commencement of this act, in relation to an establishment" means the date of bringing into force of this act in relation to such establishment.

(3) Nothing in sections 7, 8 and 9 shall apply to any establishment wherein any process is carried on by the occupier with the aid of his family or to any school established by, or receiving assistance or recognition from, Government.

**10. Disputes as to age.**—If any question arises between an Inspector and an occupier as to the age of any child who is employed or is permitted to work by him in an establishment, the question shall, in the absence of a certificate as to the age of such child granted by the prescribed medical authority, be referred by the Inspector for decision to the prescribed medical authority.

**11. Maintenance of register.**—There shall be maintained by every occupier in respect of children employed or permitted to work in any establishment, a register to be available for inspection by an Inspector at all times during working hours or when work is being carried on in any such establishment, showing—

(a) the name and date of birth of every child so employed or permitted to work;

(b) hours and periods of work of any such child and the intervals of rest to which he is entitled;

(c) the nature of work of any such child; and

(d) such other particulars as may be prescribed.

**12. Display of notice containing abstracts of sections 3 and 14.**—Every railway administration, every port authority and every occupier shall cause to be displayed in a conspicuous and accessible place at every station on its railway or within the limits of a port or at the place of work, as the case may be, a notice in the local language and in the English language containing an abstract of sections 3 and 14.

**13. Health and safety.**—(1) The appropriate Government may, by notification in the Official Gazette, make rules for the health and safety of the children employed or permitted to work in any establishment or class of establishments.

(2) Without prejudice to the generality of the foregoing provisions, the said rules may provide for all or any of the following matters, namely:—

(a) cleanliness in the place of work and its freedom from nuisance;

(b) disposal of wastes and effluents;

(c) ventilation and temperature;

(e) artificial humidification;

(f) lighting;

(g) drinking water;

(h) latrine and urinals;

(i) spittoons;

(j) fencing of machinery;

(k) work at or near machinery in motion;

(l) employment of children on dangerous machines;

(m) instructions, training and supervision in relation to employment of children on dangerous machines;

(n) device for cutting off power;

(o) self-acting machines;

(p) easing of new machinery;

(q) floor, stairs and means of access;

(r) pits, sumps, openings in floors, etc.;

(s) excessive weights;

(t) protection of eyes;

(u) explosive or inflammable dust, gas, etc.;

(v) precautions in case of fire;

(w) maintenance of buildings; and

(x) safety of buildings; and machinery.

## PART IV
## MISCELLANEOUS

**14. Penalties.**—(1) Whoever employs any child or permits any child to work in contravention of the provisions of section 3 shall be punishable with imprisonment for a term which shall not be less than three months but which may extend to one year or with fine which shall not be less than ten thousand rupees but which may extend to twenty thousand rupees or with both.

(2) Whoever, having been convicted of an offence under section 3, commits a like offence, afterwards, he shall be punishable with imprisonment for a term which shall not be less than six months but which may extend to two years.

(3) Whoever—

(a) fails to give notice as required by section 9; or

(b) fails to maintain a register as required by section 11 or makes any false entry in any such register; or

(c) fails to display a notice containing an abstract of section 3 and this section as required by section 12; or

(d) fails to comply with or contravenes any other provisions of this act or the rules made thereunder, shall be punishable with simple imprisonment which may extend to one month or with fine which may extend to ten thousand rupees or with both.

**15. Modified application of certain laws in relation to penalties.**—(1) Where any person is found guilty and convicted of contravention of any of the provisions mentioned in sub-section (2), he shall be liable to penalties as provided in sub-sections (1) and (2) of section 14 of this act and not under the acts in which these provisions are contained.

(2) The provisions referred to in sub-section (1) are the provisions mentioned below:—

(a) section 67 of the Factories Act, 1948 (63 of 1948);

(b) section 40 of the Mines Act, 1952 (35 of 1952);

(c) section 109 of the Merchant Shipping Act, 1958 (44 of 1958); and

(d) section 21 of the Motor Transport Workers Act, 1961 (27 of 1961).

**16. Procedure relating to offences.**—(1) Any person, police officer or Inspector may file a complaint of the commission of an offence under this act in any court of competent jurisdiction.

(2) Every certificate of as to the age of a child which has been granted by a prescribed medical authority shall, for the purposes of this act, be conclusive evidence as to the age of the child to whom it relates.

(3) No court inferior to that of a Metropolitan Magistrate or a Magistrate of the first class shall try any offence under this act.

**17. Appointment of Inspectors.**—The appropriate Government may appoint Inspectors for the purposes of securing compliance with the provisions of this act and any Inspector so appointed shall be deemed to be a public servant within the meaning of the Indian Penal Code (45 of 1860).

**18. Power to make rules**—(1) The appropriate Government may, by notification in the Official Gazette and subject to the condition of previous publication, make rules for carrying into effect the provisions of The act.

(2) In particular and without prejudice to the generality of the foregoing power, such rules may provide for all or any of the following matters, namely:—

(a) the term of office of, the manner of filing casual vacancies of, and the allowances payable to, the Chairman and member of the Child Labour Technical Advisory Committee and the conditions and restrictions subject to which a non-member may be appointed to a sub-committee under sub-section (5) of section 5;

(b) number of hours for which a child may be required or permitted to work under sub-section (1) of section 7;

(c) Grant of certificates of age in respect of young persons in employment or seeking employment, the medical authorities which may issue such certificate, the form of such certificate, the charges which may be thereunder and the manner in which such certificate may be issued:

Provided that no charge shall be made for the issue of any such certificate if the application is accompanied by evidence of age deemed satisfactory by the authority concerned;

(d) the other particulars which a register maintained under section 11 should contain.

**19. Rules and notifications to be laid before Parliament or State legislature.**—(1) Every rule made under this act by the Central Government and every notification issued under section 4, shall be laid, as soon as may be after it is made or issued, before each House of Parliament, while it is in session for a total period of thirty days which may be comprised in one session or in two or more successive sessions, and if, before the expiry of the session immediately following the session or the successive sessions aforesaid, both Houses agree that the rule or notification should not be made or issued, the rule or notification shall thereafter have effect only in such modified form or be of no effect, as the case may be; so, however, that any such modification or annulment shall be without prejudice to the validity of anything previously done under that rule or notification.

(2) Every rule made by a State Government under this act shall be laid as soon as may be after it is made, before the legislature of that State.

**20. Certain other provisions of law not barred.**—Subject to the provisions contained in section 15, the provisions of this act and the rules made thereunder shall be in addition to, and not in derogation of, the provisions of the Factories Act, 1948 (63 of 1948), the Plantations Labour Act, 1951 (69 of 1951), and the Mines Act, 1952 (35 of 1952).

**21. Power to remove difficulties.**—(1) If any difficulty arises in giving effect to the provisions of this act, the Central Government may, by order published in the Official Gazette, make such provisions not inconsistent with the provisions of this act as appear to it to be necessary or expedient for removal of the difficulty:

Provided that no such order shall be made after the expiry of a period of three years from the date on which this act receives the assent of the President.

(2) Every order made under this section shall, as soon as may be after it is made, be laid before the Houses of Parliament.

**22. Repeal and savings.**—The Employment of Children, Act, 1938 (26 of 1938) is hereby repealed.

(2) Notwithstanding such repeal, anything done or any action taken or purported to have been done or taken under the act so repealed shall, in so far as it is not inconsistent with the provisions of this act, be deemed to have been done or taken under the corresponding provisions of this act.

**23. Amendment of Act 11 of 1948.**—In section 2 of the Minimum Wages Act, 1948,—

(i) for clause (a), the following clauses shall be substituted, namely:—

(a) "adolescent" means a person who has completed his fourteenth year of age but has not completed his eighteenth year;

(aa) "adult" means a person who has completed his eighteenth year of age;

(ii) after clause (b), the following clause shall be inserted, namely:—

(bb) "child" means a person who has not completed his fourteenth year of age;

**24. Amendment of Act 69 of 1951.**—In the Plantations Labour Act, 1951,—

(a) In section 2, in clauses (a) and (c), for the word "fifteenth", the word "fourteenth" shall be substituted;

(b) section 24 shall be omitted;

(c) in section 26, in the opening portion, the words "who has completed his twelfth year" shall be omitted.

**25. Amendment of Act 44 of 1958.**—In the Merchant Shipping Act, 1958, in section 109, for the word "fifteen", the word "fourteen" shall be substituted.

**26. Amendment of Act 27 of 1961.**—In the Motor Transport Workers Act, 1961, in section 2, in clauses (a) and (c), for the word "fifteenth", the word "fourteenth" shall be substituted.

## THE SCHEDULE
### (See section 3)

## PART A

**Occupations.**—Any occupation connected with —

(1) Transport of passengers, goods or mails by railway;

(2) Cinder picking, clearing of an ash pit or building operation in the railway premises;

(3) Work in a catering establishment at a railway station, involving the movement of a vendor or any other employee of the establishment from one platform to another or into or out of a moving train;

(4) Work relating to the construction of a railway station or with any other work where such work is done in close proximity or between the railway lines;

(5) A port authority within the limits of any port.

(6) Work relating to selling of crackers and fireworks.*

(7) Abattoirs/Slaughter houses.**

## PART B

(1) Beedi-making.

(2) Carpet-weaving.

(3) Cement manufacture, including bagging of cement.

(4) Cloth printing, dyeing and weaving.

(5) Manufacture of matches, explosives and fireworks.

(6) Mica-cutting and splitting.

(7) Shellac manufacture.

(8) Soap manufacture.

(9) Tanning.

(10) Wool-cleaning.

(11) Building and construction industry.

(12) Manufacture of slate pencils (including packing)*

(13) Manufacture of products from agate.*

(14) Manufacturing processes using toxic metals and substances such as lead, mercury, manganese, chromium, cadmium, benzene, pesticides and asbestos.*

(15) "Hazardous processes" as defined in section 2(cb) and 'dangerous operations' as notified in rules made under section 87 of the Factories Act, 1948 (63 of 1948).**

(16) Printing as defined in section 2(k) (iv) of the Factories Act, 1948 (63 of 1948).**

(17) Cashew and cashewnut desaling and processing.**

(18) Soldering processes in electronic industries.**

*Inserted by notification No. SO. 404 (E) dated 5th June, 1989 published in the Gazette of India, Extraordinary.

**Inserted by notification No. SO.263 (E) dated 29th March, 1994 published in Gazette of India, Extraordinary.